JOURNEY THROUGH SCRIPTURE
GENESIS TO JESUS

Journey Through Scripture
Genesis to Jesus

Studying Scripture From the Heart of the Church

Kimberly Hahn and Michael Barber

PUBLISHED BY ST. ANTHONY MESSENGER PRESS
CINCINNATI, OHIO

RESCRIPT

In accord with the *Code of Canon Law*, I hereby grant my permission to publish *Genesis to Jesus* by Kimberly Hahn and Michael Barber.

Monsignor Kurt H. Kemo
Vicar General of the Diocese of Steubenville
Steubenville, Ohio
December 18, 2007

The Permission to Publish is a declaration that a book or pamphlet is considered to be free from doctrinal or moral error. It is not implied that those who have granted the Permission to Publish agree with the contents, opinions or statements expressed.

Unless otherwise noted, Scripture passages have been taken from the *Revised Standard Version*, Catholic edition. Copyright ©1946, 1952, 1971 by the Division of Christian Education of the National Council of Churches of Christ in the USA. Used by permission. All rights reserved.
(Note: The editors of this volume have made minor changes in capitalization to some of the Scripture quotations herein. Please consult the original source for proper capitalization.)

Quotes are taken from the English translation of the *Catechism of the Catholic Church* for the United States of America (indicated as *CCC*), 2nd ed. Copyright ©1997 by United States Catholic Conference—Libreria Editrice Vaticana.

Excerpts from *Vatican Council II: The Conciliar and Post Conciliar Documents, New Revised Edition*, vol. 1, edited by Austin Flannery, copyright ©1996, Costello Publishing Company, Northport, New York.

Cover design by Mark Sullivan
Cover photo: Cameraphoto Arte, Venice / Art Resource, NY
    Pittoni, Giovanni Battista (1687-1767). *Sacrifice of Isaac.*
Book design by Phillips Robinette, O.F.M.

LIBRARY OF CONGRESS CATALOGING-IN-PUBLICATION DATA

Hahn, Kimberly.
  Genesis to Jesus : studying Scripture from the heart of the church / Kimberly Hahn and Michael Barber.
      p. cm. – (Journey through Scripture)
  Includes bibliographical references.
  ISBN 978-0-86716-837-2 (pbk. : alk. paper) 1. Bible—Textbooks. 2. Christian education—Textbooks—Catholic. I. Barber, Michael, 1977- II. Title.

BS606.3.H34 2007
220.071—dc22

                              2006102670

ISBN 978-0-86716-837-2

Published by Servant Books, an imprint of
St. Anthony Messenger Press.
28 W. Liberty St.
Cincinnati, OH 45202
www.ServantBooks.org

Printed in the United States of America.
Printed on acid-free paper.

08 09 10 11 6 5 4 3 2

Contents

Introduction

"IGNORANCE OF THE SCRIPTURES," Saint Jerome famously said, "is ignorance of Christ."[1] Yet Scripture study, for many Christians, seems a daunting
task. The Bible comprises so many different books—where's the best place to
begin? It is full of disparate stories and confusing laws. It describes peoples who
lived in ancient cultures quite foreign to our own. How are Catholics to make
sense out of the Bible?

The St. Paul Center for Biblical Theology was established in 2000 with the
express purpose of developing materials to help Catholics deepen their faith
through Scripture study. Dr. Scott Hahn, the Center's founder and president,
describes its goal as "biblical literacy for lay Catholics and biblical fluency for
priests." The Center is devoted to meeting the needs of students who describe
themselves as beginners, as well as those who are advanced students or scholars.
In addition, the Center sponsors conferences and publishes the academic jour-
nal *Letter and Spirit.*

At every level of study, the Center's goal is succinctly stated in its motto:
"Reading the Bible from the heart of the Church." In sum, this phrase refers to
the Center's overall emphasis on the liturgical dimension to Scripture. It is in
the liturgy that the Bible truly comes alive. There the mysteries we hear are
made present, and we enter into them.

Scripture and liturgy go hand in hand, as the Second Vatican Council stated:
"The Church has always venerated the divine Scriptures as she venerated the
Body of the Lord, in so far as she never ceases, particularly in the sacred liturgy,
to partake of the bread of life and to offer it to the faithful from the one table
of the Word of God and the Body of Christ" (*Dei Verbum*, 21).

Furthermore, it is in the liturgy that the Church gives us a model for how to
read the Bible. How do we make sense out of the Bible? The answer is found in
the liturgy.

Taking Our Cue From Vatican II

Prior to Vatican II the Church used an annual lectionary, the book of Scripture readings used in the Church's liturgy. This former lectionary drew from a list of mostly New Testament readings. One of the most important accomplishments of the Second Vatican Council was the reform of the lectionary. In this redesign the Council Fathers revealed the Church's vision for the proper reading of Scripture. The three-year cycle we use today allows Catholics to hear much more of the Scriptures—both Old and New Testaments—read at Mass than they did before the Council.

The Council Fathers decided that on Sundays and holy days the Church would read from four biblical passages. They established a structure familiar to Catholics today: a first reading, usually an Old Testament text; a responsorial psalm, almost always taken from the book of Psalms; a second reading, drawn from a New Testament book; and finally a selection from one of the Gospels.

The fathers deliberately arranged the readings for particular Sundays and feast days to emphasize the way the New Testament fulfills the Old Testament. In fact, they demonstrated the organic unity of the two Testaments, an important theme of the Council's teaching. In the *Dogmatic Constitution on Revelation,* the Council stated: "God, the inspirer and author of the books of both Testaments, in his wisdom has so brought it about that the New should be hidden in the Old and that the Old should be made manifest in the New" (*Dei Verbum,* 16).[2]

The Council Fathers illustrated this teaching beautifully in the arrangement of the readings in the new lectionary. Take, for example, the readings assigned for the eucharistic feast of Corpus Christi, the Solemnity of the Body and Blood of Christ, in Year A. The first reading is taken from Deuteronomy 8, where Moses reminds Israel of how the Lord fed them with the manna, the bread from heaven. This reading is correlated to the Gospel reading from John 6, where Jesus describes himself as the true manna: "I am the living bread which came down from heaven.... This is the bread which came down from heaven, not such as the fathers ate and died; he who eats this bread will live for ever" (John 6:51, 58).

The new lectionary was such a triumph that many non-Catholic communities began to use it as a model for their own worship. Major ecumenical inroads were made as a result. Today we continue to pray that through reading Scripture together, the divisions in Christianity will be healed.

This Bible Study

Journey Through Scripture, the St. Paul Center's series of parish Bible study pro-grams, takes its cue from the Second Vatican Council's reform of the lectionary and follows the model the Church gives us for reading Scripture in the liturgy. *Genesis to Jesus* is the first study in the series. This particular study has spread already to many dioceses throughout the United States and is being used in many places throughout the world. It is for all kinds of students: High school students, college students and lay adult Catholics have participated in highly successful pilot programs. Blessed Mother Teresa's order, the Missionaries of Charity, have used this material as part of their religious formation.

Genesis to Jesus gives an overview of salvation history, leading participants on a pathway through the Bible. The purpose here is to help readers see the "big picture"—to discover the overarching story, the single plot, that runs through the various books of the Bible.

What is that story? It is the story of God's plan to bring all humanity into his covenant family. This study will serve as a foundation on which future studies will build.

It's helpful for a newcomer to a city to locate its landmarks, its major points of interest. Then he or she explores the various surface streets and more remote locations, moving from what is familiar to what is less familiar. In a sense this Bible study takes participants down the highway that runs through the Bible.

This study focuses on the major landmarks or "hinge" events in the story of salvation: God's covenants with creation, Noah, Abraham, Moses and David and the new covenant established by Jesus. Having completed *Genesis to Jesus,* students will have a better understanding of the story of the Bible. They will see how all of the various stories "fit" into God's plan. They then will be equipped to undertake more specialized studies and explore the "surface streets of Scripture"—studying, for example, one of the Gospels or one of the New Testament letters.

Much of *Genesis to Jesus* takes its cue directly from the lectionary. For exam-ple, on the Feast of the Immaculate Conception, the lectionary links God's promises to Eve with the Annunciation of Gabriel to Mary. Similarly, at the end of our study of God's covenant with creation, in session two, we turn from Genesis 3 to Luke 1, discussing Mary's role as the New Eve.

In order to facilitate your learning experience, this Bible study comes with a number of resources. In this booklet you will find outlines to help you follow along in each session. You need not be concerned about writing down every-thing presented, as the notes for the individual sessions—all of the biblical ref-erences and other citations—are here also. You can review the material again and again.

Each outline concludes with suggested readings to deepen your understand-ing of the material and a suggested Scripture reading to prepare for the follow-ing lesson. By reading ahead you will "stay ahead of the curve" and be well prepared for the next presentation.

Some readers may have purchased this study guide in a bookstore rather than at a *Journey Through Scripture* study program. If you would like more information about programs in your area, or if you would like to start a pro-gram, please contact the St. Paul Center for Biblical Theology, 2228 Sunset Blvd., Suite 2A, Steubenville, Ohio, 43952, phone (740) 264-9535, or visit our Web site, www.salvationhistory.com.

Alternatively, some readers may wish to use this booklet as a personal Bible study. An outline can give you an overview of where that lesson will take you. The notes then can "jump-start" your own exploration of the Scriptures.

Hearing the Voice of God in Scripture

The Second Vatican Council explained that we encounter the voice of the Lord through the reading of Sacred Scripture: "In the sacred books the Father who is in heaven comes lovingly to meet his children, and talks with them. And such is the force and power of the Word of God that it can serve the Church as her sup-port and vigor, and the children of the Church as strength for their faith, food for the soul, and a pure and lasting fount of spiritual life" (*Dei Verbum*, 21).

It is our prayer that this study will enable all of us who participate in it to hear the voice of the Father with greater clarity in Scripture, so that upon read-ing it we will proclaim: "The Word of the Lord. Thanks be to God!"

Journey Through Scripture: Genesis to Jesus

Lesson Outlines

Studying Scripture From the Heart of the Church

Emmaus Road

Jesus appears on the first Easter Sunday.

- Luke 24:13–34

Opening the Scriptures

The first thing Jesus does after rising from the dead is to teach his disciples how to read the Scriptures.

- Luke 24:26–27

Breaking the Bread

At the disciples' meal Jesus takes, blesses, breaks and gives the bread.

- Luke 24:28–31
- Luke 22:14–20: Last Supper
- Luke 24:35

The Mass Is the Key to the Word of God

The reading of Scripture in the Liturgy of the Word and the breaking of bread in the Liturgy of the Eucharist cause our hearts to be enflamed and our eyes to be opened at every Mass!

The Word of God

The "Word of God" is found in both the Scriptures and the Eucharist.

- *CCC*, 108
- John 1:14
- *Dei Verbum*, 21

The Bible and the Mass: Then and Now

- Revelation 1:3 (see Colossians 4:16; 1 Thessalonians 5:27)

Opening the Scriptures

Breaking the Bread

The Spirit of Truth

Jesus promises to send the Holy Spirit to lead the disciples into all truth.

- John 16:12–14

The Divine Author

- *Dei Verbum*, 24: "The Sacred Scriptures contain the Word of God, and, because they are inspired, they are truly the Word of God."
- 2 Timothy 3:16, 17

Theopneustos [thay ah´ new stos] means God-breathed (Greek).

- 2 Peter 1:20–21
- *CCC*, 304: God is the "Principal Author" of Scripture.

The Word Incarnate and the Word Inspired

The Word is divine and human.

As Jesus is both God and man, so Scripture is both divine and human.

- *Dei Verbum*, 11: "Since, therefore, all that the inspired authors, or sacred writers, affirm should be regarded as affirmed by the Holy Spirit, we must acknowledge that the books of Scripture, firmly, faithfully and without error, teach that truth which God, for the sake of our salvation, wished to see confided to the sacred Scriptures."

- *CCC,* 103: The Church venerates the Word written as she venerates the Body of Christ (see *Dei Verbum,* 21).

The Human Authors

Like any human book, the Bible reflects a worldview.

- *Dei Verbum,* 12: "The exegete must look for that meaning which the sacred writer, in a determined situation and given the circumstances of his time and culture, intended to express and did in fact express, through the medium of a contemporary literary form."

The Bible Is Literature

The Bible is not just one book; it's a book of books.

The Bible contains a variety of literature: poetry, prose, prophecy, narrative, proverbs, parables....

From Promise to Fulfillment

The literary meanings of the Old and New Testaments communicate historic events and saving realities (see Genesis 1:1; Revelation 21:1).

- Galatians 4:4–5
- *Dei Verbum,* 2: literary signs
- Luke 1:68–79
- Matthew 28:19–20 (see Acts 13:16–41)
- 1 Corinthians 10:1–11
- *CCC,* 117

The Old and the New

Saint Augustine said, "The New Testament is concealed in the Old and the Old Testament is revealed in the New."

Typology: Hebrews 10:1 (see John 1:29; 1 Corinthians 5:5–7)

- John 6:31–35

Typology Reveals God's Fatherly Plan
- *CCC*, 128
- *CCC*, 129
- *CCC*, 130

History as "His Story"
The Bible gives us history from God's perspective.

How to Understand Scripture
Literary Sense

Historical Truth

Divine Meaning

The Bible Is a Gift From God
The Bible is a family heirloom, passed from generation to generation.

For the Sake of Our Salvation
- 2 Timothy 3:14–15
- *Dei Verbum,* 21: "In the sacred books the Father who is in heaven comes lovingly to meet his children, and talks with them. And such is the force and power of the Word of God that it can serve the Church as her support and vigor, and the children of the Church as strength for their faith, food for the soul, and a pure and lasting fount of spiritual life."

All of Life Under the Authority of God's Word
The Bible takes the guesswork out of how we can please God.
- Psalm 119:9–11
- Deuteronomy 6:4–7 (see Nehemiah 8; Exodus 20—24)

The Holy Spirit Safeguards Interpretation
- 2 Thessalonians 2:15
- Ephesians 4:11–14
- 2 Peter 1:20

- *CCC*, 100
- *Dei Verbum*, 10: "Sacred Tradition and sacred Scripture make up a single sacred deposit of the Word of God."

Studying Scripture From the Heart of the Church

Trusting the Holy Spirit who inspires it, preserves it and empowers the Church to interpret it.

- Ephesians 1:9, 10

Saint Irenaeus

- "Understanding...consists in...showing why there were a number of covenants with mankind, and in teaching what is the character of each of the covenants" (*Against Heresies*, book 1, chapter 10, n. 3).

Salvation History = Covenant History

What we call "testament" ancient Israelites called "covenant."

Contracts and Covenants in Contrast

Covenants Make Families

For ancient Israelites, the difference between covenants and contracts is about as significant as the difference between marriage and prostitution! Throughout salvation history, God uses covenants to extend his divine family.

- Jeremiah 31:31–34 (see Ezekiel 36:28)
- *CCC*, 238

Salvation History Time Line

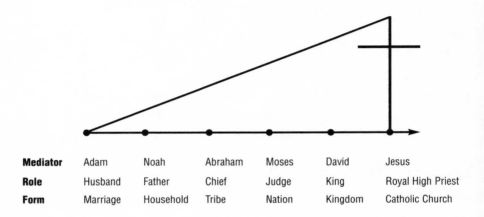

Mediator	Adam	Noah	Abraham	Moses	David	Jesus
Role	Husband	Father	Chief	Judge	King	Royal High Priest
Form	Marriage	Household	Tribe	Nation	Kingdom	Catholic Church

Where We Are Now

Salvation history is not over; it is still unfolding.

Reflection Questions for Discussion:

1. Read Psalm 1 together. What is the attitude of the psalmist toward the law? Does this surprise you? Why would the psalmist view the law with such a grateful heart and want to meditate on it all of the time (see Psalm 19:7–10)?

2. How can we increase our meditation on the law of the Lord? Would anyone like to share what practices you have found helpful in meditating on Scripture?

3. Read Ephesians 6:10–17. How is the Word of God an offensive weapon?

4. Read Psalm 119:9–11. What difference could memorizing Scripture make in our daily lives?

5. We know that Scripture teaches "without error." So what do we do when we find a passage of Scripture that seems to contradict what we know about science or seems to contradict another passage?

6. How does the Church teach us to love and to revere Scripture during the Mass?

Recommended Readings:

Genesis to Jesus, Introduction and Lesson One, pp. vii–x and 67–75

Scott Hahn, *A Father Who Keeps His Promises: God's Covenant Love in Scripture* (Cincinnati: Servant, 1998), chapter one

Dei Verbum

*CCC,** 100–109, 112–114, 128–130, 134–141

Begin to memorize the books of the Old Testament in order this week.

In preparation for the next lesson, read Genesis 1—3.

* These are paragraph numbers in the *Catechism of the Catholic Church,* not page numbers.

The Creation Covenant

The Bible's Plot = Salvation History

God's plan for salvation unfolds in the course of human events in history.
To understand salvation history, we need to understand God's covenants
with his people.

In the Beginning (Genesis 1:1–2:15)
- Jeremiah 33:25

Doctrine of Creation
The Church *does not* require us to believe:

_____

_____

The Church *does* require us to believe: *God created the world & our parents*

_____

Creation was:

_____

_____

And God Said
- Psalm 33:6–9

We know, by reading the Old Testament in light of the New Testament, that
Jesus is the Word of God by which the world was created.
- John 1:1–3 (see Colossians 1:16–17; Hebrews 1:2)

Pattern of Creation

In Genesis 1, we see the literary artistry of the author.

- Genesis 1:1, 2: In the beginning the world was

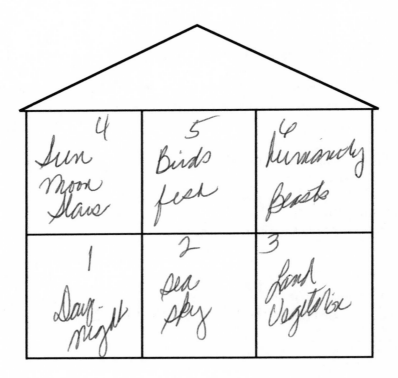

Image and Likeness = Divine Sonship

- Genesis 1:26–27
- Genesis 5:1–3
- Luke 3:38: Adam

Working for the Weekend

- Genesis 2:2, 3: The seventh day = the day of rest
- CCC, 288

Sabbath – Sign of God's Creation Covenant

Sheba [sheh vah´] means "to swear an oath" or "to seven oneself" (Hebrew).

- Genesis 21:25–32

Beer-sheba (Hebrew) translates either to "well of the ____7____ " or "well of the _oath_ ."

- Jeremiah 33:25–26
- Exodus 31:16, 17

True Meaning of the World

- Job 38:4–7

Parallels between creation and the Tabernacle (see Genesis 2:2–4; Exodus 29:43–44; 40:9; Exodus 31:12–17)

- 1 Kings 6—8

Genesis 1 and Genesis 2

Conflicting or complementary?

God calls man to be _____ over the completed temple of the world.

Genesis 1: _God the creator_   Genesis 2: _God the Father_

- Genesis 2:15 (see Numbers 7:7–8; 8:26; 18:4–5)

Adam Is the High Priest of Humanity

Adam is God's royal first-born son, high priest of humanity.

Jesus is God's Son, high priest forever.

- Romans 5:14
- Hebrews 1:6
- Hebrews 5:5; 7:15–22
- Revelation 1:6 (see 1 Peter 2:9)

Marriage Covenant in God's Plan

God created man and woman in covenant relationship (see *CCC*, 1602).

Marriage supper of the Lamb: Revelation 19:9 (see Revelation 21:1, 9; 22:17)

John Paul II

The Trinity is the divine family.

- *Puebla: A Pilgrimage of Faith* (Boston: Daughters of St. Paul, 1979), p. 86.

We Image the Divine Family

- Genesis 2:24
- Genesis 1:27

Temptation and the Fall – Making Sense of the Story

- *CCC,* 390
- Genesis 3 affirms an actual "event"—"the original fault" of Adam and Eve—that forever "marked" human history.

God Prepares Adam for the Test

- Genesis 2:16–17
- Genesis 2:23–24

Adam and Eve Are Ready

God gave Adam both natural life (human) and supernatural life (divine).

- Adam and Eve are in a state of grace (see *CCC,* 375).

The Threat of the Serpent

Nahash [nuh hawsh'] means a "serpent" or "deadly creature" (Hebrew).

- Numbers 21:6–9
- Isaiah 27:1–3
- Revelation 12:3, 9 (see *CCC,* 395)

The Test of Their Lives

The Serpent counters God's solemn declaration to Adam that the day Adam eats the forbidden fruit he will die.

Will Adam

- trust God as Father?

- exercise dominion over the beasts?

- protect his bride?

- offer his life in sacrifice?

Did Adam and Eve Die?

They lost something greater than physical life—they lost divine life, the life of grace in their souls.

- *CCC*, 403: The death of the soul

Pride and Disobedience – Failing the Test of Love

- *CCC*, 397: "Man, tempted by the devil, let his trust in his Creator die in his heart and, abusing his freedom, disobeyed God's command."

- *CCC*, 398: "In that sin man *preferred* himself to God and by that very act scorned him."

Adam and Eve lose.

God Confronts Adam and Eve

God comes to them in the garden in judgment and gives them every chance to confess their sins.

- Genesis 3:8–13

- Psalm 29:1–9 (see Psalm 46:7) — *The sound of the Lord*

Covenant Curses

- Genesis 3:15–19 — Serpent

— Woman

— Man

The First Gospel

God promises a redeemer—the *Protoevangelium*, or "first gospel" (see Genesis 3:15).

Jesus Is the New Adam
- *CCC*, 410–411: the promise of a New Adam and New Eve
- Romans 5:17–19 (see 1 Corinthians 15:21–22, 45–49; Romans 5:14)

The Power and Fear of Death Destroyed
Jesus bears the curses of the covenant as the New Adam.

- Hebrews 2:14–15
- Matthew 26:36–46
- Luke 22:44
- Matthew 27:29, 31
- Acts 5:30
- John 19:26–35

Self-Offering
Jesus is the perfect example of total self-offering.

- Luke 1:38

God's Abundant Mercy
God makes merciful provisions for Adam and Eve.

Understanding the Test
The story of the Bible is the story of God's love for his people.

God uses images of human love: parent and child, husband and wife.

Reflection Questions for Discussion:
1. Look at Genesis 1:26–28. What does it mean to say that God created man and woman "in his own image"?
2. What were Adam's missteps? His failure?
3. What were Eve's missteps? Her failure?
4. How do Adam and Eve respond when God confronts them with their sin?
5. How does God show Adam and Eve mercy?
6. How does Jesus bear the curses triggered by the sin of Adam and Eve?

Recommended Reading:

Genesis to Jesus, Lesson Two, pp. 77–84

A Father Who Keeps His Promises, chapters two and three

CCC, 68–70, 355–360, 369–385, 388–390, 395–405, 410–412, 703–704, 1602, 2172, 2568

Keep working on memorizing the books of the Old Testament.

In preparation for the next lesson, read Genesis 4—11.

the 2nd covenant

Noah and a Renewed Creation

Introduction

Though the sin of Adam and Eve sends humanity into a downward spiral of wickedness, God does not abandon the human family.

- *CCC*, 55
- Galatians 4:4: fullness of time

The Two Seeds

Conflict between the two seeds: the seed of woman (righteousness) and the seed of the Serpent (wickedness).

- Genesis 3:15
- Genesis 3:24; 4:8

From the beginning of time, people have come into God's presence to worship through sacrifice, and their hearts are open to God.

- Hebrews 11:4
- 1 John 3:11, 12

God Confronts Cain

As with Adam and Eve, God asks Cain questions to bring him to repentance.

Like Adam and Eve, Cain has excuses.

- Genesis 4:9–15

Covenant curse: an extreme form of fatherly punishment, designed to lead hardened sinners to repent

----

Imagine the grief of Adam and Eve: not only is their son
murdered, but he was killed by their beloved firstborn,
who now has been banished.
How bitter are the fruits of their sin!

Adam's Family Divided

The two seeds and sons now emerge as two family lines in conflict.

Shem: "name"; reputation, family or glory (Hebrew)

- Genesis 4:26

Cain and the wicked line (see Genesis 4:17, 19–24)

Seth and the godly line (see Genesis 4:26)

- Genesis 5:24
- Hebrews 11:5
- Genesis 5:1–3

Mixed Marriages

The Sethite line is compromised through mixed marriages with the
Cainite women.

- Genesis 6:1, 2: men of renown = the men of the name (*shem*)
  (see Genesis 6:4)
- Genesis 6:5, 6

Saved Through Water

All the righteous sons have fallen away except for Noah, who is chosen
and called to serve as the covenant mediator between God and man.

- Genesis 6:12–13

Hamas [hah mahs´] means "violence"; notion of terrorism (Hebrew)

- Genesis 6:5, 9, 14–22

Noah bears witness to God's impending judgment (_____) and his covenant mercy (_____) (see Hebrews 11:7; 2 Peter 2:5).

....

Noah and his wife have done something remarkable: in a world filled with depravity, they have raised a godly family. Noah's family believed God's Word through him. For years they assisted in getting the ark and then the animals ready for God's judgment. They knew the whole culture was against them and, even more, against God. Yet they had the courage and fortitude to obey God's Word.

....

A New Creation

The covenant is renewed.

- Genesis 6:18

Berith [beh reet´] means "covenant" (Hebrew).

Heqim [heh keem´] means "to establish" or "to renew" (Hebrew).

Parallels between the flood narrative and the Creation account:

- Genesis 1:2
- Genesis 7:11
- Genesis 7:10; 8:4
- Genesis 8:10–12
- Genesis 7:2
- Genesis 5:29
- Genesis 8:20–22

Salvation History Time Line

(*see* page 8)

A New Adam

Noah as royal priest (see Genesis 9:1–6)

Adam	Noah
Genesis 1:28	Genesis 9:1
Genesis 1:28	Genesis 9:2
Genesis 2:15	Genesis 9:20
Genesis 3:6–7	Genesis 9:21
Genesis 1:26	Genesis 9:6

God's covenant with Noah

The Table of Nations

The table reveals God's fatherly perspective and purpose for humanity.

- Genesis 10:1, 32

One Big Broken Family (Again)

Through Noah's faithful firstborn son, Shem, God continues to build his covenant family.

The unrighteous line of Ham is the source of moral corruption and conflict.

Dr. Hahn: "Israel was enslaved by Egypt, ensnared by Canaan, oppressed by the Philistines, annihilated by Assyria, and exiled by Babylon" (*A Father Who Keeps His Promises*, p. 90).

The Tower of Babel

The descendants of Noah bring down God's judgment, confusing their language.

- Genesis 11:1–9
- *CCC*, 57

The Covenant With Noah

God extends his covenant with Noah to all people until the time of Christ.

- *CCC*, 58

A warning (see *CCC*, 701, 1219)

A Flood of Comparisons

The covenant with Noah points us to the sacrament of baptism.

- 1 Peter 3:20–21
- *CCC*, 701
- *CCC*, 1219

Literary Framework of Genesis 1—11

The literary framework links Adam and Eve to Noah, Abraham and the rest of salvation history. *seth - good descendants*

Narrative Structure

Ham - evil descendants

Human history is told from God's perspective as the story of the human race as the family of God.

Toledoth [to´ leh dote] refers to generations (Hebrew).

- Genesis 2:4; 5:1; 6:9

Conflict within the human family (see Genesis 3:15; 4—5; 10—11)

It is very challenging for us to live in the world and resist worldliness, to live in the midst of a godless culture and maintain a clear witness to godly living. How can we live our citizenship in the City of God while we sojourn in the City of Man?

Reflection Questions for Discussion:

1. Read 1 Peter 3:18–22. What is the relationship between the saving of Noah's family on the ark and our being saved through baptism?

2. How do we have an assurance of faith based on our baptism without committing the sin of presumption?

3. What does the story of Noah and the flood teach us about justice? about mercy?

4. What can we learn about living our faith even when it is difficult and countercultural?

5. What can we learn from the example of Noah and Mrs. Noah about raising a godly family in an ungodly culture? How can it be done?

Recommended Readings:

Genesis to Jesus, Lesson Three, pp. 85–92

A Father Who Keeps His Promises, chapter four

CCC, 56–58, 68–71, 701, 1218–1220, 2569

Begin to memorize the books of the New Testament while reviewing the books of the Old.

In preparation for the next lesson, read Genesis 12—22, Hebrews 11:1–22

Abraham: Our Father in Faith

And God Blessed Them....

The blessing of the covenant is given and received through the family (see Genesis 1:22, 28; 2:3; 9:1, 26–27).

Fatherly Blessing

God the Father promises to bless Abraham and through him all humanity (see Genesis 9:11).

- Genesis 12:1–3

The covenant blessing passed on through Shem will now come through his descendant, Abraham.

Salvation Time Line

(*see* page 8)

In this lesson we will examine God's covenant with Abraham.

Adam triggers covenant curses by failing to obey God. Conversely, Abraham secures God's blessing.

The Three Promises of Genesis 12:1–3

God promises Abraham three blessings:

Abram Goes in Faith

Abram leaves with part of his clan and begins a nomadic life, obeying God's call.

- Genesis 12:4–9 (see Genesis 17:4)
- Hebrews 11:8–10

The Tests of the Blessed

Abraham's life reveals that the road to blessing is paved with trials and temptations.

- Genesis 12: Famine, exile and temporary "loss" of his wife
- Genesis 13: Family strife and division
- Genesis 14: Wars
- Genesis 15: Unfulfilled promises
- Genesis 16: Marital discord
- Genesis 17: Surgery (circumcision)
- Genesis 18—19: Supernatural destruction of Sodom and Gomorrah
- Genesis 20: Another temporary "loss" of his wife
- Genesis 21: More family strife and division
- Genesis 22: The ultimate trial of a father: the offering of his beloved son
- Hebrews 6:13–17

God Blesses Abram Through Melchizedek

- Genesis 14:17–20: After the trials God fulfills his promise to bless Abram through Melchizedek, the first man in Scripture to be called a priest.

Melchizedek [Mel keez´ uh dek] means "righteous king" (Hebrew).

Melchizedek prefigures Christ.

Salem [suh lem´] means "peace" (Hebrew).

- Hebrews 6:19—7:2

The First Covenant Oath — *make a great nation*

God swears a covenant oath to give Abram a son.

- Genesis 15:1–6
- Genesis 15:13–16: God swears that Abram will be a father to innumerable descendants.
- Genesis 15:7–21 (see Genesis 12:2) — *sealed the 1st covenant*

Abram's Other Son

As time goes by, elderly Abram and his wife, Sarai, grow impatient and decide to take matters into their own hands.

- Genesis 16:1–6

Sarai tells Abram that he should take her Egyptian handmaid and have a son (Ishmael) through her.

The Second Covenant Oath *promise of a son - Issac*

- Genesis 17:1–8: Abram > Abraham "father of a multitude"
- Genesis 17:15: Sarai > Sarah "great mother"
- Genesis 17:16: kings of peoples shall come from her
- 2 Samuel 7:9
- Genesis 17:17–19

Ishmael will not be the chosen heir. God promises that Abraham will have a son but must circumcise himself and all the males in his tribe. *on the 8th day of birth*

Good news = Genesis 17:21

Bad news = Genesis 17:9–14, 26

Isaac and Ishmael

One year later Isaac is born. Sarah asks Abraham to banish Hagar and Ishmael (see Genesis 21:8, 10–14).

The Final Covenant Oath *Bless + deliver all nations through the seed of Abraham (Issac) Christ*

God asks Abraham to sacrifice his son on Mount Moriah.

- Genesis 22:1–4
- Genesis 22:3–18: God renews his covenant with Abraham.

Sowing Seeds of Future Blessings

- Genesis 22:18: God swears to bless all the nations through Abraham's seed (see Genesis 3:15). *Christ*

The woman did not bring salvation to the world; her "seed," Christ, did. Salvation will come not through Abraham but through his seed.

- Matthew 1:1
- Galatians 3:14–17

The Obedience of Abraham and Isaac

In Abraham the curse of the Fall is partially reversed, and through Abraham's "seed" the curse will be fully reversed.

The ancient rabbis explained that this story is as much about Isaac's self-offering as it is about Abraham's faithfulness.

Aqedah (ak´ uh duh) refers to the "binding" of Isaac (see Genesis 22:6, 9).

Jewish tradition explained that Isaac asked to be "bound" so not to struggle against his father.

The Only Beloved Son of the Father

A foreshadowing of the sacrifice of the true only beloved Son of the Father (see Genesis 22:2; John 3:16; Romans 8:32)

- John 19:17 (see Genesis 22:6)
- Hebrews 11:19 (see Genesis 22:4; 1 Corinthians 15:4)

My Beloved Son

Genesis 22 is read in connection with Jesus' transfiguration.

- Mark 9:7
- Genesis 22:2

God Will Provide Himself the Lamb

In Christ Abraham's words came true (see Genesis 22:8).

Mount Moriah, a mountain range found outside Jerusalem, is part of salvation history (see 2 Chronicles 3:1).

- John 1:29

Three Promises Strengthened by Three Oaths

The three promises of Genesis 12:1–3 are later strengthened by three covenant oaths:

land + nation, kingship world
nation great name family

- Genesis 15
- Genesis 17
- Genesis 22

These three covenant oaths are fulfilled by:

1) _____

and _____

2) _____

and _____

3) _All nations will be blessed_

and _____

The Elder Shall Serve the Younger *all older sons fail*

Abraham's son, Isaac, has two sons, Esau and Jacob. Jacob is chosen over Esau.

God chooses the weaker, younger brother to show that his plans are fulfilled through his power.

- Romans 9:11, 16

The Rest of the Story

Isaac's son Jacob is later renamed "Israel" and has twelve sons, who become the twelve tribes of Israel—a nation.

Genesis ends with the story of Joseph.

- Genesis 48:21: God's promise to Joseph (see Genesis 15:13, 14)

Reflection Questions for Discussion

1. Discuss Abraham's example of faith. What trials did he face?

2. How does he take matters into his own hands, and what difference does that make?

3. What is the relationship between blessing and trials for modern Christians?

4. What does the story of Abraham's offering of Isaac teach us about God's fatherly sacrifice for us?

5. What does Isaac's self-offering teach us about Jesus' self-offering?

6. From what did Abraham detach in order to follow God's plan for his life? And how is that an example for us?

Recommended Readings:

Genesis to Jesus, Lesson Four, pp. 93–100

A Father Who Keeps His Promises, chapters five and six

CCC, 59–61, 72, 144–146, 164–165, 705–706, 1080–1081, 1819, 2570–2573, 2592

Review the Old and New Testament books in order.

In preparation for the next lesson, read Exodus 1—4; 12; 19; 24—25; 32; Ezekiel 20:1–26

Moses and the Israelites

The Story of God's Firstborn Son

Genesis reveals that salvation history is the story of God's family.

Exodus recounts how the families described in Genesis become nations.

Just as God's firstborn sinned, so the people of Israel fail to realize their calling as firstborn among nations (see Exodus 4:22).

Abraham's Family Line

- Genesis 35:9–13

Abraham is the father of Isaac, who is the father of Jacob = Israel.

Jacob/Israel is the father of twelve sons, who become the twelve tribes of Israel.

Twelve tribes become enslaved in Egypt.

Salvation History Time Line

(*see* page 8)

God establishes his covenant with a nation—Israel—through Moses.

Liberty or Death

Abraham's descendants were to become slaves, but God would deliver them from bondage and bring them to the Promised Land.

- Genesis 15:13–14
- Exodus 1:8–12
- Exodus 2:23–25

Moses' Early Life
Pharaoh orders the slaughter of all male Hebrew babies (see Exodus 1:15–22).

Moses means "taken from the water" (Hebrew).

- Exodus 2:1–10
- Exodus 2:11–16

The Call of Moses
- Exodus 3:1–8: The burning bush
- Exodus 3:9–10, 18–20: God tells Moses his plan.

God calls Israel his "firstborn son" among the nations.

- Exodus 4:21–23

The Gods of Egypt
Israel was to sacrifice to the Lord the very animals the Egyptians worshiped as gods.

- Exodus 8:25–27

More Than Political Liberation
The Israelites were actually in the worst kind of bondage—spiritual bondage.

- Ezekiel 20:6–9
- Exodus 7:16

The Plagues of Egypt
When Pharaoh refuses to let the people go, God responds by sending ten famous plagues on Egypt. Let's look at a few:

- Numbers 33:3, 4 (see Wisdom 11:15–16)
- see Exodus 7:14–25: Nile River to blood
- see Exodus 8:1–15: plague of frogs
- see Exodus 9:4: land of Goshen spared

- see Exodus 9:1–7: cattle destroyed
- see Exodus 10:21–29: three days of darkness

The Tenth Plague

The Lord will send his angel of death to slay the firstborn sons in Egypt and the firstborn male offspring of all livestock.

- Exodus 11:1, 4–9
- Exodus 12:1–14: Passover instruction
- Exodus 12:28–36

Baptized Into Moses

The Lord comes down and cares for his people, though they complain against him.

Red Sea parted (see Exodus 14:10–14, 16–18, 21–31).

Thirst (see Exodus 15:22–25)

Hunger (see Exodus 16:1–4, 35)

Thirst (see Exodus 17:1–7)

New covenant foreshadowed (see 1 Corinthians 10:1–6)

....

This was an issue of trust—would the people of God trust God to provide for their needs?

Would their attitude be one of contentment —God will provide (see Genesis 22:8, 14)?

Or would it be one of contentiousness—murmuring against God, assuming he will not provide?

....

The First Covenant With Israel

Finally the Lord brings his people to Mount Sinai.

- Exodus 19:5, 6: holy nation and royal priesthood
- Ten Commandments (see Exodus 20:1–17; 32:15, 16)
- Book of the covenant (see Exodus 21:1–23:33)
- Exodus 24:3–8: twelve pillars
- Covenant ratified with a meal (see Exodus 24:9–11)

The Tabernacle

Moses receives a vision of a heavenly pattern for the tent of worship—the mobile temple (see Exodus 25:9).

- Exodus 24:15–18
- Hebrews 8:5 (see Isaiah 6; Revelation 21—22)

God's purpose in delivering Israel

The Golden Calf

While Moses is on the mountain, Israel reverts to the idolatrous practices of the Egyptians.

- Exodus 32:1–6, 25

By worshiping the golden calf, Israel succumbs to the three major temptations used by the devil since the dawn of time: money, sex and power.

God "Remembers" His Oath

Because Israel breaks the covenant, Israel deserves death.

- Exodus 3:10
- Exodus 32:7, 10, 13–14

If God destroys the Israelites, he'll kill Abraham's descendants, through whom God promised to bless all nations (see Genesis 22:18).

Of course, God doesn't forget his oath. He swore it to Abraham; he knew Israel would need it.

Israel Breaks the Covenant
- Exodus 32:15–19

Moses descends the mountain and, upon seeing the idolatry of Israel, smashes the tablets of the Ten Commandments.

- Exodus 32:26–29

The Levites respond, kill the idolaters and are ordained.

God's Second Covenant With Israel

Israel has revealed that they are still in spiritual bondage to the gods of Egypt.

Consequently, they are given an elaborate code of ritual purity laws, recounted in Leviticus.

The Levitical Priests

No longer is Israel a nation of priests (see Exodus 19:6; Numbers 1—6).

The Book of Leviticus explains to the priests the purity laws for the priests (see Leviticus 1—10) and the laws the Levites are to teach the people (see Leviticus 11—26).

The Book of Numbers

The Israelites arrive at the border of the land promised to them, but they refuse to enter into it, fearing those who inhabit the land.

- Galatians 3:19
- Numbers 13:30—14:10

Deuteronomy

Because of their sinfulness God gives Israel a "lower law" (see Numbers 25; Matthew 19:8).

Deuteronomy is not promulgated in the words of God but through the words of Moses.

Deuteronomy means "second law" (Hebrew).

- Exekiel 20:25
- Galatians 3:24

Plans for the Sanctuary

In Deuteronomy, Moses gives Israel instructions to reconquer the land promised to Abraham, Isaac and Jacob.

The goal of Deuteronomy—as of Exodus—is more than political independence.

- Deuteronomy 12:10–11

Jesus as the New Moses

Jesus' life reveals many parallels with the story of Moses:

- is born during the reign of a ruthless king who kills other Hebrew male children
- finds safety in Egypt
- is called back to his birthplace after exile
- passes through waters and goes into wilderness
- fasts for forty days and forty nights
- turns water into wine and later into blood
- teaches from a mountain
- goes up a mountain with three companions
- offers heavenly bread and spiritual drink
- appoints twelve leaders, then an additional seventy
- teaches about the Passover Lamb
- leads God's people out of spiritual bondage

The New Passover

God uses the historical events in the Old Testament to prefigure Christ's salvation in the New Testament.

- 1 Corinthians 5:7–8
- Matthew 26:26–28

Reflection Questions for Discussion

1. Read Exodus 3:13–4:17. What excuses did Moses give God so that he would not have to do what God asked him to do?

2. How do we make excuses to not follow God's lead in our lives?

3. What is the difference between contentment and contentiousness? Read Proverbs 21:9, 19.

4. How did the people respond to the God-appointed leader Moses?

5. How are we to respond to the authorities God has placed in our lives, such as our bishops and the pope?

6. How did the people of Israel demonstrate their lack of trust in the Lord?

7. Are there ways we murmur against the Lord, assuming he will not provide for our needs? What can we do to counter that lack of trust?

Recommended Reading:

Genesis to Jesus, Lesson Five, pp. 101–109

A Father Who Keeps His Promises, chapters seven, eight and nine

CCC, 62–64, 72, 1221–1222, 2574–2577, 2593, 2598

In preparation for the next lesson, read 2 Samuel 6—7; Isaiah 9, 53; Jeremiah 31.

The Covenant With David

Joshua: The Promised Land: Entrance and Conquest

Joshua leads (see Joshua 3, 4, 6–12, 13–21).

- Joshua 24:14-15

Judges: The Conquest Continues

Judges lead Israel gradually in a series of victories.

Three-D cycle: Disobedience, Defeat, Deliverance

- Judges 21:25

1 and 2 Samuel: The Conquest Completed

The conquest is completed by the kings of Israel.

- 1 Samuel 8:1–9

Saul, First King of Israel

- 1 Samuel 10:1: Samuel anoints Saul as the first king (see 1 Samuel 9:2).

King Saul Falls

Two major errors cost Saul greatly (see 1 Samuel 13:8–14).

- 1 Samuel 15:1–3, 8–9
- 1 Samuel 15:20–23 (see 1 Samuel 16:11–13)

David Rises to Power

David defeats Goliath and becomes a part of Saul's household (see 1 Samuel 17; 20).

Saul realizes that David is God's anointed one (see 1 Samuel 23:15; 24).

King Saul and his sons perish (see 1 Samuel 31; 2 Samuel 1:19–24; 9).

David Wants to Build a House for God

David fulfills the conditions of the Deuteronomic covenant and desires to build a temple.

- Deuteronomy 12:10, 11
- 2 Samuel 7:1–3
- Psalm 132:1–3, 11–18

God Will Build a House for David

David has too much blood on his hands.

- 2 Samuel 7:11–16

Bayith [buy eet´] means "house" (Hebrew). There are three levels of meaning: family, dynasty, temple.

The Covenant Time Line

God establishes the kingdom of David.

A Kingdom of Priests

The Davidic kingdom is God's means of extending his covenant.

Israel fails to achieve their calling as a kingdom of priests (see Exodus 19:6).

- 2 Samuel 6:14, 17–19: David aspires to priestly service.

David as Liturgical Leader

- 1 Chronicles 28:19

David organizes Israel's worship and leads the procession of the ark of the covenant (see 1 Chronicles 15–16, 23–27).

David makes thank offerings a prominent aspect of Israel's liturgical life (see Leviticus 7:12–15; Psalm 22; Psalms 69; 100; 116).

- 1 Chronicles 16:37–40

Todah [to dah´] means "thankgiving" (Hebrew); referred to Israel's thank offerings

Jesus as the New David

The Davidic covenant, the final covenant between God and Israel, is the prototype of the new covenant.

2 Samuel 7:8–17	Luke 1:32–33
9: a great name	32: He will be great
14: he shall be my son	32: and will be called the Son of the Most High
16: establish the throne	32: the Lord…will give…the throne of his father David
16: forever	33: he will reign over the house of Jacob for ever

Seven Primary Features of the Davidic Covenant

First: The Son of David is the Son of God.

God swears that David's son will be his son.

- Psalm 2:7
- Psalm 89:26–27

Israel	David	Jesus
Exodus 4:22	Psalm 89:27	Hebrews 1:6
Exodus 19:6	Psalm 110:1–4	Hebrews 8:1

Second: The Davidic king is a "Messiah."

The Davidic king is crowned in order to be enthroned.

Mashiach [mah she´ ah] means "anointed one" or "Messiah" (Hebrew) (see 1 Samuel 16:13).

Psalm 89:19–21 (see 1 Kings 1:32–40; 2 Kings 11:12; 23:30; 2 Chronicles 23:11)

Christos [kris´ tos] means "anointed one" or "endowed with the Spirit" (Greek) (see Matthew 1:1).

Mark 1:9–11 (see Luke 1:5; John 1:32; 2 Samuel 5:4; Luke 3:23).

Third: The Davidic kingdom is international.

The kingdom is not limited to nations around the land of Canaan (see 1 Chronicles 11:11–12; Psalm 72:8–11; Psalm 2:8).

- Matthew 28:19

Jesus instructs the apostles to make disciples of "all nations."

- Acts 1:8
- Acts 13:47

Fourth: The Davidic kingdom is located in Jerusalem.

Jerusalem becomes the political capital for the Davidic kingdom; Mount Zion will be the spiritual center of Israel.

- Psalm 87:5

Fifth: The Temple of Solomon

The temple is where God chose for his name to dwell (see 1 Kings 8:27–30).

Moses (see Exodus 25:9)

David (see 1 Chronicles 28:19; 1 Kings 5)

- Hebrews 8:5

Eben shetiyah [eh vahn shet´ ee yah] means the foundation stone of the temple (Hebrew), where Abraham offered Isaac.

- 2 Chronicles 3:1 (see Genesis 22:2; Matthew 7:24; 12:42; 16:18)
- John 2:19–21

Sixth: Wisdom of Solomon

- 1 Kings 3:5, 9–14, 28

Solomon asks for the wisdom to be able to govern a vast empire justly (see 1 Kings 4:29–30).

Solomon builds and dedicates the temple (see 1 Kings 8).

- 1 Kings 4:34: Solomon instructs all nations (see 1 Kings 10:1–10).

Solomon's wisdom literature includes Proverbs, Ecclesiastes, Song of Solomon, Wisdom of Solomon.

Jesus' words of wisdom (see 1 Corinthians 1:30; John 14:26)

Seventh: An Everlasting Kingdom

David's kingdom is everlasting: 2 Samuel 7:13 (see Psalm 89:36–37).

The Davidic king is caught and his sons are killed before him (see 2 Kings 25:7).

Secondary Features of the Davidic Covenant

Solomon establishes a throne for the queen mother (see 1 Kings 2:19).

- Matthew 16:19: The prime minister is designated the chief steward of the kingdom (see Isaiah 22:15–25).

The *todah* becomes the primary liturgy (see Leviticus 7:11–21; 1 Chronicles 16).

The Psalms and the Thank Offering

- Psalm 50:14–15: David writes many of the Psalms, especially *todah* (with three steps).
- Psalm 69:30–31: Israel learns to offer afflictions to God in thanksgiving.

Eucharistia [you car ist ee´ uh] means "thanksgiving" (Greek).

David's Sin

- 2 Samuel 11:1: David lingers at home instead of leading his troops in battle.

"Thou Art the Man!"

- 2 Samuel 12:1–7, 10–15

Nathan confronts David with his sins, and David repents deeply.

- Psalm 51:10–12: psalm of confession

From Moses to David

Moses	David
Mount Sinai in the wilderness	Zion/Jerusalem
Exclusive; national	Inclusive; international
Tent for Israel's worship	Temple for all to worship
Sin offerings	Thank offerings
Torah: Law of God	*Hokmah:* Wisdom of Solomon

Fulfilling Abraham's Covenant

After Solomon's coronation God's three promises to Abraham are fulfilled (see Genesis 12:2, 3; 17:6–8; 22:17, 18).

- 1 Kings 4:20, 21
- 2 Samuel 7:9
- Psalm 72:17

Solomon's Later Failures

Moses gave three warnings for the future king of Israel: don't multiply weapons, wealth or wives.

Moses' Warnings	Solomon's Failures
Deuteronomy 17:16: weapons	2 Chronicles 9:25, 28
Deuteronomy 17:17: wealth	1 Kings 10:14, 23–25, 27
Deuteronomy 17:17: wives	1 Kings 11:1–4

Fall of the Kingdom

Because of Solomon's sin, God allowed the kingdom to be divided (see 1 Kings 11:9–40; 2 Kings 25; Ezra 1:2, 3).

←——— 930 BC ——————— 722 BC ——————— 586 BC ——→

Death of Solomon   Israel destroyed by Assyrians   Judah exiled by Babylon

The Prophets

The prophets foretell God's restoration of the Davidic kingdom.

- Isaiah 9:1–7 (see Isaiah 53:5, 10, 12)
- Jeremiah 31:31–33

Reflection Questions for Discussion

1. What does it mean "to obey is better than sacrifice"?
2. What does it mean to be a man or woman "after God's own heart"?
3. How does David honor the Lord's anointed, even when he is being hunted down to be killed by King Saul? What insight does that give us?
4. Are there ways that we linger, allowing opportunity for sin, rather than choosing decisively to reject the temptation?
5. How can we explain the importance of the kingdom of God to children who live in a society with an elected government?
6. What place do we have in the kingdom of God?

Recommended Readings

Genesis to Jesus, Lesson Six, pp. 111–120

A Father Who Keeps His Promises, chapters ten and eleven

CCC, 709, 2578–2580, 2594–2596

In preparation for the next lesson, read Matthew 1—7; 16; 24—28.

Jesus: Fulfillment of the Promises

Salvation History Time Line

In Christ we have a new creation, a new exodus and a new kingdom.

Birth and Deliverance

Through his life and ministry, Jesus is revealed as the New Moses.

Tested in the Desert

Fasting for forty days and forty nights.

Jesus rebukes the devil with Deuteronomy 6—8 in Matthew 4:1–11.

- Deuteronomy 8:2–3: Do not live by bread alone.
- Deuteronomy 6:13: Serve God alone.
- Deuteronomy 6:16: Do not tempt the Lord your God.

Covenant Law Given on a Mountain

After his forty-day fast, Jesus begins his public ministry by declaring the new covenant law on a mountain (see Matthew 5—7).

- Matthew 5:17

He internalizes and intensifies the law of Moses.

- John 1:17
- John 5:39, 46–47

	Jesus	Moses
Signs and Miracles		
Water turned into wine	John 2:1–11	Water into blood Exodus 7:19
Miraculous food John 6:32–35	John 6:4–14	Exodus 16:2–30
Miraculous cure	Matthew 8:2–3	Prays for cure

New Leaders Appointed

Coworkers to assist in caring for God's people: twelve, seventy and three

The twelve	Matthew 10:1–8	Numbers 13
The seventy	Luke 10:1	Numbers 11
The three	Luke 9:28	Exodus 24:1

Opposed and Rejected by Israel's Leaders

	Matthew 9:32–34 (see John 5:18)	Numbers 16:3

Transfigured on a Mountain

The Mount of Transfiguration underlines Jesus' role as the new Moses.

Exodon [ex´ o don] means "departure" or "exodus" (Greek).

Jesus speaks to Moses and Elijah about his *Exodon*.

	Luke 9:28–31, 34	Exodus 24:1, 15; 34:29

The Passover Celebrated

The Gospels show us how Jesus celebrates the Passover and transforms it into the Eucharist.

	Luke 22:7–13, 19; Matthew 26: 28, 38, 41	Exodus 12:14, 42 (see Exodus 24:8)

The Passover Fulfilled

Jesus fulfills the Passover through his passion and death.

- John 19:14–16: The sixth hour

- John 19:23–36; Exodus 12:46: The lamb without blemish

- John 19:23: The priest's seamless garment

- John 19:29: Hyssop branch used to sprinkle the blood (see Exodus 12:21–22)

- Luke 22:19, 20: The blood of the covenant (see Exodus 29:12; Leviticus 4:7)

- Isaiah 53:3–12

The Eucharist and Calvary are inseparable—one and the same sacrifice.

What Jesus begins in the Upper Room he concludes on the Cross.

The Resurrection

The work of salvation is not complete with Jesus' death for our sins.

- Romans 4:24–25 (see *CCC*, 651–655)

- 1 Corinthians 15:3–5, 12–14, 16–17, 20–22, 42–45

The Resurrection is the climax of God's covenant plan.

The New Adam in the Garden

Jesus rises from the dead and appears in a garden (see John 20:15).

Jesus' obedience undoes Adam's disobedience (see Luke 22:39–44).

Jesus bears the covenant curses (see Genesis 3:10, 18–19; Luke 22:44; Matthew 27: 29, 31; Hebrews 12:2).

Jesus' cross is the Tree of Life (see Acts 5:30; John 19:26–35; Deuteronomy 21:23; Galatians 3:13, 14).

Jesus bears the covenant curses redemptively.

On the Third Day

On the third day the Father receives his only beloved Son back from the dead, fulfilling the oath he swore to bless all nations through his seed.

- Genesis 22:2, 4, 8 (see Hebrews 11:19)

Matthew's Gospel of the Kingdom

The apostles understand that Jesus is *the* Son of David come to restore the Davidic kingdom (see Matthew 1:1; 2:5; 1 Samuel 16:4).

Jesus the "Christ"

Jesus is the "anointed one," the true Davidic King.

He's baptized by a Levite (see 1 Kings 1:34; 2 Kings 11:12; 23:30; 2 Chronicles 23:11).

He's declared to be the Son of God (see Matthew 3:17; Psalm 2:7).

- Matthew 4:23: Preaching "the gospel of the kingdom"

The Sermon on the Mount (Matthew 5—7)

And he urges people to seek the kingdom above all in Matthew 5—7.

- Matthew 5:3, 10: Jesus teaches the law of the kingdom.
- Matthew 6:9–15: Jesus gives us the Our Father.
- Matthew 6:33: Jesus urges the people to seek the kingdom above all.
- Matthew 7:24; 12:42: Jesus' wisdom

Seven Kingdom Parables

Wisdom is revealed through proverbs and parables. The kingdom is of the greatest value but is hidden in the world.

Jesus teaches seven kingdom parables in Matthew 13:

- Sower (3–9)
- Weeds Among the Wheat (24–30)
- Mustard Seed (31–32)
- Yeast (33)
- Hidden Treasure (44)
- Pearl of Great Value (45–46)
- Dragnet (47–50)

The Church is not an earthly political institution and is made up of saints and sinners.

Israelites and Gentiles

Jesus ministers to Gentiles as well as Israelites (see Matthew 8:5–13; 15:21, 22–28).

- Matthew 15:31

The Keys of the Kingdom

"Keys" in the Old Testament symbolized Israel's prime minister's authority in the kingdom. When Jesus gives Peter the keys, he uses similar language.

- Matthew 16:18–19

- Isaiah 22:20, 22

Greater Than Solomon

Jesus was the *Son* of David coming to the *City* of David to restore the *kingdom* of David.

- Matthew 21:6–7, 9–10 (see Mark 11:10; Luke 19:38)

- 1 Kings 1:38–40

Thy Kingdom Come

The meal Jesus is celebrating is intimately connected to the coming of the kingdom.

- Luke 22:16–19, 27–30

The only kingdom covenanted in Scripture is the kingdom of David.

The New *Todah*

Todah [to dah´] means "thanksgiving" (Hebrew).

David moves the thank offering, the *Todah*, to the center of Israel's liturgical life (see Psalm 50:14–15).

The Last Supper is a *Todah* meal.

Jesus prays a *Todah* psalm on the cross (see Psalm 22:1, 6–8, 14–18, 22–28).

Through the Eucharist we share in the *Todah* and enter into the kingdom, and God's covenant plan is accomplished.

The Book of Acts

After the Resurrection Jesus appeared to the apostles and spoke to them for forty days about "the kingdom of God."

- Acts 1:3–8
- Psalm 72:8

The apostles will be sent out to the City of David, the royal territory, the area of the ten northern tribes and "to the end of the earth."

The Davidic King Enthroned, the Kingdom Restored

With the coming of the Spirit at Pentecost, Jesus has established his kingdom in the heavenly Jerusalem.

Peter shows how the Resurrection and Ascension represent the fulfillment of the Davidic covenant.

- Acts 2:29–36
- Psalm 89:3–4
- Psalm 132:11
- Psalm 110:1

The Apostles Preach the Kingdom

The apostles deal with the admission of gentiles into the Church.

- Acts 15:13–19 (see Amos 9:11, 12)
- Romans 1:1–4

The Heavenly Jerusalem

The Resurrection fulfills God's oath to David to establish his kingdom forever (see 2 Samuel 7:13; Psalm 89:3–4).

- Hebrews 12:22–24a, 28

Through the Eucharist we enter the kingdom.

Through his Ascension Jesus transfers the kingdom to heaven.

God's covenant plan for salvation history is accomplished.

Where the King is, there is the kingdom!

Where the Eucharist is, there is the King!

Reflection Questions for Discussion

1. The devil tried to twist Scripture when he tempted Jesus; yet Jesus knew Scripture so well that he untwisted Satan's lie and responded with other verses. How can we grow in relying on God's Word to strengthen us in difficult times and to deliver us from temptation?

2. Read Galatians 2:20. What does it mean to be "crucified with Christ"?

3. Read Philippians 1:21. What does it mean?

4. Read Mark 8:34–35. How can we live this truth?

5. How do we proclaim the kingdom?

6. How can we grow in love for our Lord in the Eucharist?

Recommended Readings

Genesis to Jesus, Lesson Seven, pp. 121–129

A Father Who Keeps His Promises, chapters 12 and 13

CCC, 430, 436, 651–656, 695, 697, 2599–2616

Journey Through Scripture: Genesis to Jesus

Student Notes

STUDENT NOTES

STUDENT NOTES

STUDENT NOTES

STUDENT NOTES

STUDENT NOTES

_____

_____

_____

_____

_____

_____

_____

_____

_____

_____

_____

_____

_____

_____

_____

_____

_____

_____

_____

_____

_____

_____

_____

_____

_____

_____

_____

_____

STUDENT NOTES

STUDENT NOTES

_____

_____

_____

_____

_____

_____

_____

_____

_____

_____

_____

_____

_____

_____

_____

_____

_____

_____

_____

_____

_____

_____

_____

_____

_____

_____

_____

_____

_____

_____

STUDENT NOTES

STUDENT NOTES

Journey Through Scripture: Genesis to Jesus

Lessons

Studying Scripture From the Heart of the Church

Welcome to the first lesson in *Journey Through Scripture.* This lesson is a Bible study about the Bible. Why should Catholics study sacred Scripture? And what framework provides the clearest picture for understanding God's provision for his children's salvation? We begin this investigation by turning to an event that happened on the first Easter Sunday (see Luke 24:13–35).

The Emmaus Road

Two disciples leave Jerusalem and travel on the road toward Emmaus. They have faith in Jesus but are confused about the events surrounding his crucifixion. Jesus joins them on their journey, but they do not recognize him. They even talk with this "stranger" about Jesus and the events that occurred that very weekend, culminating in the death of Jesus. Then the Lord opens the Scriptures and explains them to the two disciples.

The first thing Jesus does after rising from the dead is to teach his disciples how to read the Scriptures. He explains that the Christ had to suffer and then enter his glory and that all of the Scriptures point to Christ (see Luke 24:26–27). The disciples are amazed yet still do not recognize the stranger walking with them as Jesus.

As the three draw near to Emmaus, the disciples urge Jesus to stay with them. With his consent they sit for a meal. Jesus *takes, blesses* and *breaks* bread; then he *gives* it to his disciples. Immediately this reminds the disciples of Jesus' actions at the Last Supper (see Luke 22:14–20), where he *took, blessed, broke* and *gave* bread to his disciples. This was the first celebration of the Mass, where the disciples discovered Christ's real presence in the breaking of the bread.

As soon as the disciples recognize Jesus, he disappears. The disciples are amazed. Now they understand all that Jesus has done with and for them. "Did not our hearts burn within us while he talked to us on the road, while he opened to us the Scriptures?" (Luke 24:32). Immediately they return to Jerusalem.

The Mass: The Key to the Bible

Notice this vital connection: the *reading* of Scripture caused the disciples' *hearts* to burn; the *breaking* of bread caused their *eyes* to be opened (see Luke 24:30–31). Likewise, through the *reading* of Scripture in the Liturgy of the Word and the *breaking* of bread in the Liturgy of the Eucharist, *our* hearts are enflamed and *our* eyes are opened—at every Mass!

Muslims refer to Islam as a religion of the book. "Christianity," the *Catechism of the Catholic Church* states, "is the religion of the 'Word' of God,...'not a written and mute word, but the Word which is incarnate and living' (St. Bernard, S. *missus est hom.* 4, 11: PL 183, 86). If the Scriptures are not to remain a dead letter, Christ, the eternal Word of the living God, must, through the Holy Spirit, 'open [our] minds to understand the Scriptures' (Cf. *Lk* 24:45)" (*CCC*, 108).[1] The Word is a Person, Jesus Christ (see John 1:14).

Through Jesus the fullness of God's revelation comes to us. The Word of God is revealed both in the Scriptures and in the Eucharist (see *Dei Verbum*, 21). Thus we have a personal encounter with the Word of God in every Mass. We receive the *written* word of God along with the *eucharistic* Word of God!

The Bible is a liturgical book. Its content is liturgical, and its context is the liturgy. At every stage of God's plan, God's people respond to his covenant love by offering sacrifice and entering into his presence as a worshiping community. As we shall see, from the Book of Genesis, which describes Adam as a priest, to the Book of Revelation, which reveals Christ as the true heavenly High Priest, liturgy is the major theme of Scripture.

Not only is the Bible about liturgy, but its books were assembled to be read in the liturgy. The apostles urged believers to read their apostolic letters in church (see Colossians 4:16; 1 Thessalonians 5:27; Revelation 1:3). This is what it means to read the Bible from the heart of the Church.

Many believers through the centuries could not own a copy of the Bible, either because they lived before any Scripture was written or before the invention of the printing press. However, believers *did* have access to the Scriptures through the readings at Mass.

Likewise the Church gives us the whole Bible to be read at Mass so that, like the early disciples, *our* hearts will burn when we have the Scriptures opened to us. First we hear Old Testament readings from Moses and the Prophets; then we hear New Testament readings, from Jesus and the apostles.

Following the reading and explanation of Scripture, Jesus wants us to receive what the disciples received: *himself!* During the Mass the priest *takes* the bread. The priest then *blesses* the bread with Jesus' very words. He also *breaks* the bread. Finally the priest *gives* the bread to us. Like the disciples, we "recognize" and receive the risen Jesus "in the breaking of the bread" (see Luke 24:31, 35).

The Word Incarnate and the Word Written

After Jesus ascends to the Father, the promised Holy Spirit descends upon the disciples at Pentecost. He is the "Spirit of truth" sent to lead the apostles "into all the truth" (John 16:13). How does he do that? The Holy Spirit *inspires* Scripture, *safeguards* the Church's interpretation of the Scripture and *continues to guide* Jesus' disciples into all truth through the Church.

Dei Verbum states that "the Sacred Scriptures contain the Word of God, and, because they are inspired, they are truly the Word of God" (*Dei Verbum*, 24). This kind of "inspiration" does not refer to artistic creativity as we might understand it. Rather, all Scripture is *theopneustos* [thay ah´new stos], which means "God-breathed" (see 2 Timothy 3:16).

The Bible, unlike any other book in the entire world, is the Word of God in the very words of God and men. It is divinely inspired, without reducing its human authorship to mechanical dictation. The human authors, moved by the Holy Spirit, wrote the Scriptures (see 2 Peter 1:21), so the sacred books bear the authors' own personal styles and individual perspectives. At the same time, since God is the primary Author behind the human authors, everything the Bible teaches is without error (*Dei Verbum*, 11).

The Word is both *divine* and *human*. Just as the Word of God Incarnate took on all the weaknesses of human flesh yet without sin (see Hebrews 4:15), so the Word of God inspired comes to us with all the limitations of human language yet without error. This is why the Church venerates the Word written just as she venerates the Body of Christ (see *Dei Verbum*, 21).

The Bible is not just one book; it is a book of books. It contains a variety of literature: poetry, prose, prophecy, narrative, proverbs, parables and more. Its authors exhibit literary artistry, though their backgrounds and educations varied. They were shepherds, fishermen, princes (Moses was trained in Pharaoh's house), warriors, kings and even a Pharisee (Saint Paul). Incredibly, though these authors differ in many ways and cross many places, times and cultures, they share a unifying plot—the overarching story—of God's plan of salvation for us unfolding in history.

Promise and Fulfillment

Unlike the modern, secular approach to history, the Bible gives us history from God's perspective: God's Word reveals God's saving work. *Scripture gives us the drama of the history of salvation.*

Structurally the Bible is divided into two parts: the Old Testament and the New Testament. Scripture *begins* with Creation (see Genesis 1:1); it *ends* with the passing away of this world and the coming of a "new heaven" and a "new earth" (see Revelation 21:1). At the *center* of the drama, however, is the *cross* of Jesus (see Galatians 4:4–5). Salvation history is a "two-part" story that presents the story of the world *before* Jesus (the promises of God) and the story of the world *after* Jesus' life, death and resurrection (the fulfillment of God's promises).

Scripture is literature, but it is not *just* literature. The words—the "literary signs"—communicate historical realities. *Dei Verbum* states: "The works performed by God in the history of salvation show forth and bear out the doctrine and realities signified by the words; the words . . . proclaim the works, and bring to light the mystery they contain. The most intimate truth which this revelation gives us about God and the salvation of man shines forth in Christ" (*Dei Verbum*, 2).

God writes the world as men write words. He gives us signs that stand for realities. He even uses historical realities to represent greater realities. For example, the Exodus events foreshadow Christ's work of redemption.

Throughout the Old Testament God promises his children a savior who will deliver them from their sins. He provides various "saviors," such as Noah, Moses, the judges, King David and others, who in fact provide a kind of deliverance. God also uses them to prefigure *the* Savior.

Throughout the New Testament God reveals the *fulfillment* of his promises. Jesus is *the* Savior of the world who was promised to the Israelites in the Old Testament (see Luke 1:68–79). Jesus commissions his apostles to restore his divine family (see Matthew 28:19–20); in turn, the apostles proclaim him to be the fulfillment of God's promises to the fathers (see Acts 13:16–41). They read the Old Testament in light of the New and the New Testament in light of the Old (see, for example, 1 Corinthians 10:1–11).

Furthermore, the *Catechism* states that "thanks to the unity of God's plan, not only the text of Scripture but also the realities and events about which it speaks can be signs" (*CCC*, 117). Thus the Old Testament *people* and *events* prefigure and point to the New Testament *Redeemer* and His saving *mysteries*. There are literary clues throughout the Bible that convey the texts' meaning.

Saint Augustine clarified that the New Testament *lies hidden* in the Old and the Old Testament is *unveiled* in the New. His insights into the unity of Scripture through this pattern of "concealment-revelation" is known as *typology*. He faithfully taught what the early Church fathers had seen: Christ was foreshadowed in the Old Testament by "types."

The Old Testament "fore-*shadows*" New Testament *realities*. For example, in the Old Testament an unblemished lamb was offered as a Passover sacrifice; in the New Testament Jesus is the "Lamb of God, who takes away the sin of the world" (John 1:29; see 1 Corinthians 5:7b). Likewise, in the Old Testament the people of Israel ate miraculous bread (called "manna") in the wilderness; in the New Testament Jesus is the Bread of Life, "the true bread from heaven" (John 6:31–35). Further, Hebrews 10:1 refers to the sacrificial laws, which assisted the people of God in the Old Testament yet were only a shadow of the true form of the reality revealed in Christ's sacrificial offering. Many more examples of typology will follow throughout this study.

Typology "discerns" God's fatherly works in the Old Testament, which point to—and are fulfilled in—*Jesus* in the New Testament (see *CCC*, 128). Typology shows us that the meaning of the events contained in the Old Testament are "inexhaustible" (*CCC*, 129). Further, typology points to the ongoing "dynamic movement" toward the fulfillment of God's fatherly plan (*CCC*, 130).

We are not merely *students* of God's work in the past, nor are we *spectators* of this "dynamic movement" from the outside. Quite the contrary: We intimately *participate* in God's saving plan. In a very real sense, we are standing in the "stream" of salvation history.

The Bible: A Gift From God

Throughout time God is working to bring us salvation. God's perspective on history *is* salvation history! At the heart of salvation history lies the covenants, and the history of salvation is the history of God's covenants.

In order to understand the Bible, we investigate the *literary sense*, the *historical truth* and the *divine meaning* of sacred Scripture. The literary sense has to do with the literary forms, figures of speech and customs used by the sacred authors. The literary sense leads us to historical truth, which reveals the way God is directing the course of history.

Finally, we see the divine meaning of Scripture. We see that history is really "his story" and that God uses certain historical people and events to foreshadow Christ and his work.

The Bible is a family heirloom, passed from generation to generation. It is a treasure to be valued and shared. It was written for the sake of our salvation (see 2 Timothy 3:14–17). In the Scriptures God comes down to our *human* level to raise us up to his *divine* level.

> In the sacred books the Father who is in heaven comes lovingly to meet his children, and talks with them. And such is the force and power of the Word of God that it can serve the Church as her support and vigor, and the children of the Church as strength for their faith, food for the soul, and a pure and lasting fount of spiritual life (*Dei Verbum*, 21).

The Bible takes the guesswork out of how we can please God. The Bible expresses the ancient truth that all of life is under the authority of God's Word (see Psalm 119:12–16): family life (see Deuteronomy 6), worship (see Nehemiah 8) and social institutions (see Exodus 20—24).

Religare [ray lih gaw´ ray] is the Latin root word of *religion*. It means "to bind together." Everything for the ancients—culture, history, the economy, diplomacy—was bound together by religion.

If we want to know how to care for a car, we need to read the owner's manual. If we want to know how to become a child of God and live in a way that pleases him, we need to read "Our Father's Manual," the Bible.

The Holy Spirit Safeguards Interpretation

Saint Paul writes, "So then, brethren, stand firm and hold to the traditions which you were taught by us, either by word of mouth or by letter" (2 Thessalonians 2:15). "Word of mouth" refers to what Saint Paul taught the people through oral tradition—through teaching, preaching and worship. "By letter" refers to what Saint Paul wrote to the people. Saint Paul binds his hearers to "hold fast" to both *oral* and *written* instruction.

Yet it is not enough to have oral and written instruction; it has to be interpreted well. Misinterpretation is a real danger (see Ephesians 4:11–14). In the Catholic Church we have not only God's word but also a faithful interpretation—preserved by the Holy Spirit—of God's Word (2 Peter 1:20–21). Instead of fracturing into thousands of denominations that disagree on many beliefs, we have the deposit of faith, which no one can change. The Holy Spirit empowers the magisterium—the bishop of Rome and the bishops united with him—to serve the people of God by faithfully preserving and proclaiming the full revelation of God (see *CCC*, 100).

"Sacred Tradition and sacred Scripture make up a single sacred deposit of the Word of God" (*Dei Verbum,* 10). Tradition is alive because it is the faithful handing down of revelation from Christ through the apostles' preaching and writing. It is living and dynamic, especially in the liturgy. The Scriptures are also living and dynamic (see Hebrews 4:12). Though there were many human authors of Scripture, there is one primary Author, God, who is the Source of that unity. We must trust the same Holy Spirit who inspired sacred Scripture to empower the Church to interpret it. "For [the Father] has made known to us in all wisdom and insight the mystery of his will, according to his purpose which he set forth in Christ as a plan for the fulness of time, to unite all things in him, things in heaven and things on earth" (Ephesians 1:9–10).

Salvation History Is Covenant History

The great early Church father Saint Irenaeus recognized the need for studying salvation history in terms of the covenants. "Understanding...consists in...showing why there were a number of covenants with mankind, and in teaching what is the character of each of the covenants."[2] The Old and New Testaments point to the old and new covenants. (What we call "testament" the ancient Israelites called "covenant.") The story of salvation is recorded as a sequence of covenants that God makes with his people.

Most people think that a covenant is the same thing as a contract. This is *not* true: Covenants are *much more* than mere contracts. Covenants and contracts both establish relationships, but the *types* of relationships they establish are very different.

Contracts are made with a *promise;* covenants are sworn with an *oath.* Contracts are signed in *our* name; covenants are sealed in *God's* name. Contracts exchange *goods and services;* covenants exchange *persons.* Contracts are *temporary;* covenants are *permanent.*

Covenants establish the strongest type of interpersonal communion: family or kinship bonds. In short, the difference between a *covenant* and a *contract* is about as significant as the difference between *marriage* and *prostitution!*

A covenant is a sacred family bond in which persons give themselves to one another in loving communion. God's covenants establish us as his family (see Ezekiel 36:28). He is our heavenly Father because of his covenant with us (see *CCC,* 238). We will examine in this Bible study a series of covenants God established with his family.

The first covenant was made with *Adam and Eve* as *husband and wife.* The second covenant was made with *Noah,* who was the head of a *household.* The third covenant was made with *Abraham,* who was the *chieftain* of an extensive *tribe.* The fourth covenant was made with *Moses,* who was *judge* over the *nation* of the twelve tribes of Israel. The fifth covenant was made with *King David,* who ruled the *kingdom* of Israel.

And finally, *Jesus* establishes the new covenant, the worldwide (catholic) kingdom of God. Salvation history reaches its goal in Christ: all things are united to him (see Ephesians 1:10). This covenant invites all people to be received into the family of God through the Catholic Church, so that all nations will be restored into his divine covenantal family through and in Jesus Christ.

Salvation history is not a thing of the past; it is still unfolding. We are still in the "flow" of salvation history. The rest of this study will examine God's plan for salvation and our place in it.

Review Questions for Personal Study

1. What do we learn when we approach the Bible as ancient religious literature?

2. What difference does it make when we approach it as salvation history?

3. How is biblical history different from secular history? How are they alike?

4. How does typology unify the Old and New Testaments?

5. What is the difference between a covenant and a contract?

6. How does understanding who God is help us understand why God works through covenants in salvation history?

7. What are the key elements common to the narrative of the road to Emmaus, the Last Supper accounts and the Catholic celebration of the Mass?

Recommended Verses to Memorize

Hebrews 4:12

2 Peter 1:20

2 Timothy 3:16–17

Psalm 119:9, 11

The Creation Covenant

Salvation history is the "plot" of the Bible, the story of God's plan for human salvation unfolding in the course of human events. But if we want to understand salvation history, we need to understand God's covenants with his people.

This second lesson examines Creation, the Fall and God's promise of redemption. What did God create and why? Why did Adam and Eve fall into sin? How did God promise to redeem his fallen sons and daughters?

In the Beginning

In Genesis 1:1–2 we read about God's calling the world into existence. Not only does he create the world, but he also establishes a covenant with his creation. Jeremiah 33:25 refers to God's "covenant with day and night." God did not create us because he was lonely or bored; as Father, Son and Holy Spirit, he created us to be his family.

Many people approach Genesis 1 and 2 in terms of a "religion versus science" debate. They often forget to read the text as the ancients would have read it. If readers impose current questions and historical situations on the text of Scripture, they miss the whole point of the account.

The Catholic Church teaches that we are not bound to believe that God created the earth in six twenty-four-hour days. However, the Church teaches that we must believe that God created the world, that he created our first parents and that they existed with him for a time in a state of original justice, happiness and innocence before their fall into sin.

Genesis 1 was not written to tell us *how* the world was created. Rather, it was written to tell us *what* was created and *why* it was created. Creation was the deliberate, purposeful act of a loving God.

In the Creation account God says, "Let there be…," and things come into being (Genesis 1:3, 6, 14). God does what he says; when he speaks, things happen. Creation occurs because of God's word (see Psalm 33:6–9). Reading the

Old Testament in light of the New, we know that Jesus is the Word of God by which the world was created (see John 1:1–3; Colossians 1:16–17; Hebrews 1:2).

Genesis 1:2 states that in the beginning the world was "without form and void." God changes this: he gives the world forms (*realms*) and fills the void (with *rulers*). Please look at the following from the first chapter of Genesis:

Days 1–3: God creates the *realms*:

Day 1: *day* and *night* (1:3–5)

Day 2: *sky* and *sea* (1:6–8)

Day 3: *land* and *vegetation* (1:9–13)

Days 4–6: God fills these realms with their *rulers*:

Day 4: *sun, moon* and *stars* (1:14–19)

Day 5: *birds* and *fish* (1:20–23)

Day 6: *beasts* first (1:24–25) and then the *human* to rule over all as the king of creation (see 1:26–28; Psalm 8).

After each day God says that his work is "good" (1:4, 10, 18, 21, 25). But after the *sixth* day, the day of creating mankind, God says that his work is "very good" (1:31).

Genesis 1:26–27 states that humans are made in the "image and likeness" of God. What does this mean? We find a literary clue in Genesis 5:1–3: Adam was made in the likeness of God, and Adam's son, Seth, was made in Adam's "own likeness, after his image." We can conclude from this that "image" and "likeness" refer to sonship. Thus Adam was "the son of God" (Luke 3:38).

The Sabbath

After God creates man and woman, the Scriptures tell us, he ordains the day of rest (see Genesis 2:2). Upon first glance this day of rest can be a little perplexing. Does the all-powerful God *need* to rest? No, he is not tired. The seventh day finishes God's design for creation. God blesses and hallows the seventh day to give us a gift—a holy day of *rest* from our labor and a call to *worship* him as members of his covenant family. Thus creation is the "first and universal witness to God's all powerful love (Cf. *Gen* 15:5; *Jer* 33:19-26)" (*CCC*, 288).

The seventh day seals God's covenant with creation. He swears a covenant oath. The Hebrew word for swearing an oath is *sheba* [sheh vah´], which literally means "to seven oneself." God "sevens" time into seven days to consecrate creation. The Sabbath is "a perpetual covenant" (see Exodus 31:16–17).

God's Sabbath is the climax of the Creation account. Through it God calls man and woman to something far more glorious than "ruling" creation: God calls them to interpersonal communion with him. The world is not just a place of work; it is also a place of *worship,* a holy dwelling place where God himself is present, where his people worship and offer sacrifice.

Scripture describes Creation as the building of a home or temple (see Job 38:4–11). Solomon builds the temple in seven years and consecrates it in the seventh month, on the seventh day of a seven-day feast, offering seven petitions (see 1 Kings 6—8). In the temple the Holy of Holies is truly the dwelling place of God; the Garden of Eden is described in terms similar to those describing the inner precincts of the temple (see Genesis 2:8–14). Once God completes the temple of the world, he calls man to be a priest-king over it.

Two Creation Accounts

Genesis 1 and 2 record two accounts of Creation. These are not two conflicting accounts; they are complementary accounts with different emphases.

In Genesis 1 God the *Creator* makes a cosmic home or temple for himself. His final creation—man and woman—he makes in his image, and he calls them to imitate him (see verse 28). In Genesis 2 God works as *Father.* He lovingly fashions man from the dirt of the earth, breathes life into him, creates a garden paradise for him and creates a spouse for him from his very side. God commands man to "till . . . and keep" the garden (Genesis 2:15), a call to priestly sacrifice in the garden sanctuary.

Adam is God's royal firstborn son, the high priest of humanity. In ancient Israel the father, as head of his family, was a priest who offered sacrifices and performed acts of worship on behalf of his household. This priesthood was passed down from father to firstborn son, who inherited the mantle of the authority of the family to lead the people to be holy. Jesus—as the "new Adam" (Romans 5:14)—calls his people, the Church, to be "a holy nation" and "a royal priesthood" (1 Peter 2:9; see Revelation 1:6).

Not only does God create man and woman in a covenant relationship with him, but he also creates them in covenant union with each other. They are joined as one in the covenant of marriage. God establishes marriage as a sign of his covenant love for us.

In a very real sense the Trinity is the divine family, and the image of the Triune God is reflected in our natural families. In marriage two become one (see Genesis 2:24), and the one they become is so real that nine months later you might have to give it a name! More than a sign, marriage is an image of who God is. The human family is created to image the Trinity, the divine family.

Temptation and Fall: Making Sense of the Story

Man's fall into sin is a very puzzling thing. The *Catechism* gives us three important things to remember when examining man's temptation and fall: (1) "The account of the fall in Genesis 3 uses figurative language"; (2) "but [the account] affirms a primeval event, a deed that took place *at the beginning of the history of man* (Cf. *GS* 13 §1)"; (3) "revelation gives us the certainty of faith that the whole of human history is marked by the original fault freely committed by our first parents (Cf. Council of Trent: DS 1513; Pius XII: DS 3897; Paul VI: AAS 58 (1966), 654)" (*CCC*, 390). Though the account in Genesis 3 is written more like poetry than journalism, it affirms an actual event—the "original fault" of Adam and Eve—that forever marks human history.

From the very beginning God alerts Adam and his helpmate Eve that there is a *danger*. Adam should "keep" or guard the garden (see Genesis 2:15); this implies that there is something to guard against! God also gives Adam a *limitation* or *restriction*: Adam can eat of every tree of the garden except one (see Genesis 2:16–17). Furthermore, God gives Adam a *warning*: if Adam disobeys and eats of the forbidden tree, he will die that day (see Genesis 2:17). Death has to be meaningful (understood) and dreadful (fearing the loss of life), or the boundary would be meaningless to Adam.

When God breathes life into Adam, he gives him more than he gave any other creature: God gives Adam the grace of divine sonship. He gives Adam *natural life* and *supernatural life*.

Adam and Eve are created in a state of grace (see *CCC*, 375). They live in harmony with God, with each other and with all of creation. They are not prone to sin, nor are they simple-minded or inadequate to the test God gives them. Quite the contrary: they are intelligent and upright people who live in right relationship with God.

Along Came a Serpent

We've all seen Bible story images of a long, thin snake slithering around an apple tree. It is important to note, however, that the Hebrew word for serpent is *nahash* [nuh hawsh´], which is a much more dangerous animal than the garden-variety snake. *Nahash* refers to an extremely deadly and dangerous creature (see, for example, Numbers 21:6–9; Isaiah 27:1; Revelation 12:3, 9). Once we see the nature of the serpent that confronts Adam and Eve, we see the *serious challenge* and *grave threat* Adam faces in guarding the garden and his wife (see *CCC*, 395).

The Serpent speaks to Eve, but he addresses Adam also. (The Hebrew word for "you" is plural.) The Serpent directly contradicts God's solemn warning to Adam about the forbidden fruit: "You will not die" (Genesis 3:4). This temptation is a test.

Adam's test involves four questions: (1) As a *son*, will Adam trust God as Father enough to obey? (2) As *king*, will Adam exercise dominion over the beasts and drive the Serpent out of the garden? (3) As *husband*, will Adam protect his bride? (4) As *priest*, will Adam—if need be—offer his life in a sacrifice of love and obedience? In short, will Adam fear a loss of *supernatural* life more than a loss of *natural* human life?

Adam fails the test: He does not trust in his heavenly Father. He fails to guard the garden, and the Serpent gains entrance. Further, Adam is *silent* when he should speak. Then Adam allows his wife to lead him into sin, instead of leading her into righteousness. Finally, Adam refuses to offer himself to God; he prefers himself to his Creator (see *CCC*, 397–398).

God Confronts Adam and Eve

God comes to Adam and Eve in the garden, not in a leisurely stroll but in judgment. They hear the powerful "sound" of the Lord (see Genesis 3:8; Psalm 29:3–9; 46:6), and they are afraid. Instead of running to the Lord, they hide.

In Genesis 3:9–13 God asks Adam and Eve four questions: (1) "Where are you?" (2) "Who told you that you were naked?" (3) "Have you eaten of the tree of which I commanded you not to eat?" (4) "What is this that you have done?" (3:8–13).

The all-powerful and all-knowing God surely knows the answers to these questions. But he wants Adam and Eve to face the reality of the grave sin they have committed. He gives them every chance to confess their sins and to be reconciled to him. Rather than facing their sin, however, Adam and Eve make excuses and blame others—even God (3:12–13).

God turns to the source of the trouble: the Serpent. He *curses* the Serpent with humiliation and destruction. God also *prophesies enmity* between the Serpent and the woman, between his offspring and hers (see Genesis 3:14–15).

God then *punishes* the man and woman. Childbirth will be painful. Relationships will be marred by sin. Work will be toil; it will not always be fruitful and instead will bring forth thorns and thistles. Even the ground will be cursed. Finally, physical death will be inevitable for all (see Genesis 3:16–19).

While Adam and Eve don't die physically in the garden, they do die spiritually. That day they lose God's divine life in their souls. This spiritual death is far worse than any physical death. This is the original mortal sin: the "death of the soul (Cf. Council of Trent: DS 1512)" (*CCC*, 403).

Adam and Eve lose their innocence and intimacy with God. Furthermore, their harmony with each other and with creation is lost. Seduced into trying to be like God without God, they exercise freedom that plunges them—and us!—into slavery and death (see *CCC*, 398). They discover their nakedness and are ashamed.

God shows mercy to Adam and Eve. He covers their nakedness by making them garments out of animal skins, thus making the first sacrifice of animals to cover the shame of his children. Then he drives them out of the garden, and he posts cherubim at the entrance so that they will not be tempted to reenter and seal their damnation by eating of the Tree of Life (see Genesis 3:21–22).

The First Gospel

God does not give up on his fallen son and daughter, however. He promises a Redeemer who will save his children, who will set right the wrong of Adam and Eve. The early Church fathers understood this promise as the "first gospel" (or the *Protoevangelium*) (see *CCC*, 410). The Fathers also understood the "seed of the woman" to be a reference to the Virgin Birth, since "seed" (*sperma*) comes from the man rather than the woman.

God's promise of a redeemer is the promise of a "New Adam" and a "New Eve" who will do what the first Adam and Eve failed to do (and undo what the first couple did) (see *CCC*, 410–411). The *New Adam* will be the one who will achieve victory over the Serpent. The *New Eve* will be his mother, the one who gives birth to the Redeemer. Just as death comes into the human race through the sin of the first Adam and Eve, so new life will come through the victory of the New Adam and the New Eve, Jesus and Mary (see Romans 5:17–21; 1 Corinthians 15:21–22, 45–49).

Sin enters the world through the "fear of death" (Hebrews 2:14–15); for Adam fears natural death over supernatural death. In contrast, Jesus takes our human nature so that through his death he can destroy the devil, who has the power of death. Jesus' death, then, delivers all of us from lifelong bondage to sin, to which we succumb because of the fear of death.

Jesus bears the curses of the covenant as the New Adam. He goes into a garden (see Matthew 26:36–46), and his sweat is like drops of blood (see Luke 22:44). However, unlike the first Adam, Jesus faces the fears of suffering and death; he chooses to trust his heavenly Father: "Father, if thou art willing, remove this chalice from me; nevertheless not my will, but yours, be done" (Luke 22:42).

Jesus' crown of thorns (see Matthew 27:29) harkens back to the thorns and thistles of Adam's fate. Like Adam and Eve, Jesus is reduced to nakedness (see Matthew 27:31, 35). Jesus dies on the cross, which was referred to as the "Tree of Life" in the early Church (see Acts 5:30). Finally, falling into the sleep of death, his bride—the Church—is formed from his side (see John 19:34).

Jesus gives us the perfect example of total self-offering when he lays down his life for us on the cross. Unlike the first Adam, Jesus yields his will completely in trust to his heavenly Father. He lays down his life for his bride, the Church. Through the Last Adam, what was lost through the sin of the first Adam is restored. Even more, we now become partakers of the divine nature, since we have been given Jesus' divine life.

Church tradition has always seen Mary as "the New Eve." In contrast to the first Eve's disregard of God's commands, Mary offers herself freely to the will of God: "Behold, I am the handmaid of the Lord; let it be to me according to your word" (Luke 1:38).

The story of the Bible is the story of God's love for his people. Just as Adam and Eve are united in marriage on the seventh day, so God wants to be united to his people in a "nuptial" or marriage-like (covenantal) bond.

We hardly can grasp God's love for us in human language. So here, in the first pages of the Bible, the Word of God uses the most powerful images of human love imaginable—that of parent and child, that of husband and wife.

Covenant love requires total self-giving: God gives himself to his people, and his people give themselves to him. This kind of love images the life-giving love of the Trinity. And since God destined us to share in his divine life, we need to learn to love as he does. From him we learn how to give ourselves fully—how to sacrifice ourselves—for each other and, most importantly, for him.

We can say that the Bible tells the story of God's raising us as his family from infancy to adulthood. Little by little he guides us, chastises us, woos us and prepares us to be fit for the wedding supper of the Lamb of heaven. He calls us to divine, heavenly union with him, which can be symbolized best by marriage—the most ecstatic and intimate of human relationships.

This is our heavenly calling, our supernatural end.

Review Questions for Personal Study

1. How is God's creation like the tabernacle and the temple?

2. How is Adam both a royal firstborn son and a priest?

3. What is the first promise that a savior will redeem the human race?

4. Read Romans 5:12–21. How does Saint Paul contrast the old Adam with the New Adam, Christ?

5. What are some practical ways I can draw strength from God to resist temptation and avoid sin?

6. How can I grow in an attitude of repentance when I commit sins?

7. Have I tried to "hide" from God? Have I refused to acknowledge my need for his mercy?

Recommended Verses to Memorize

Genesis 1:1–2

Genesis 1:26

Genesis 3:15

Noah and a Renewed Creation

This third lesson examines how God renews with Noah his Creation covenant. We look more closely at the narrative structure of Genesis 1—11. And we see how Christ fulfills in a new creation the covenants made with Adam and Noah.

Cain's Sin

In the last lesson we looked at the first covenant in salvation history, the covenant in Creation with Adam and Eve. Though the sin of Adam and Eve sent humanity into a downward spiral of wickedness, God did not abandon the human family. God promised redemption through Christ "when the time had fully come" (Galatians 4:4). It is only in Christ that God's covenant plan for creation is fulfilled at last.

As forewarned in Genesis 3:15, throughout human history there is ongoing conflict between the two seeds, the seed of the *woman* (righteousness) and the seed of the *Serpent* (wickedness). Adam and Eve have children after God expels them from his presence; immediately the "enmity" between the two seeds becomes evident in their sons.

From the beginning of time, people have come into God's presence to worship through sacrifice and to open their hearts to God. Adam and Eve's sons— Cain and Abel—offer sacrifices. God accepts Abel's sacrifice (see Hebrews 11:4), but he has no regard for Cain's offering (see 1 John 3:11–12). This greatly angers Cain.

God warns Cain to guard his heart, to resist the temptation that is trying to master him. Tragically, however, Cain defies God, gives in to envy and murders his brother (see Genesis 4:7–8).

Just as God confronted Adam and Eve after the Fall, he questions Cain in order to bring him to repentance: "Where is Abel your brother?...What have you done?" (Genesis 4:9, 10). Like his parents, Cain has excuses. He refuses to confess, and he goes on to accuse *God* and others of injustice (see Genesis 4:13–14).

Previously God cursed the Serpent and the ground but not the humans involved, not Adam and Eve (see Genesis 3:14–19). Now God curses Cain (see Genesis 4:10–12). The ground will not yield fruit because Cain has defiled it by soaking it with the innocent blood of his brother. Furthermore, Cain is driven "east" of Eden, to be a fugitive in the land of Nod (which means "wandering"). Banished and ostracized, Cain has made himself a marked man (see Genesis 4:14).

God's covenant curses are not a kind of divine mean-spiritedness. A covenant curse is an extreme form of fatherly punishment, designed to lead hardened sinners to repentance. God answers Cain's dismay with the promise, "If any one slays Cain, vengeance shall be taken on him sevenfold" (Genesis 4:15). This illustrates what always has been true: God doesn't punish us because he stops loving us; he punishes us because he *can't* stop loving us!

Adam's Family Divided

Following the loss of Abel in death and Cain in banishment, Adam and Eve have another son, Seth. Through Seth a righteous family line develops. The two seeds and sons—Cain's and Seth's—now emerge as two family lines in conflict.

Cain and the Wicked Line. Cain has a son and names him Enoch. Cain builds a city and names it after his son. The fact that Cain names a city after his son is evidence of his desire to glorify himself (see Genesis 4:17).

Seven generations from Adam we see the full flowering of evil in Cain's line. Lamech—a descendant of Cain—takes two wives. He violates God's plan for the marriage covenant in creation through bigamy. He is also defiant, violent, vengeful and murderous (see Genesis 4:19, 23–24).

Seth and the Righteous Line. Through Seth's family proper worship is restored. They "called upon the name (*shem*) of the LORD" (Genesis 4:26). Here *shem* refers to God's glory rather than one's own. This phrase refers elsewhere to sacrificial worship (see Genesis 12:8).

In the seventh generation from Adam we see the full flowering of righteousness in Enoch. This descendant of Seth has a close relationship with God (see

Genesis 5:24; Hebrews 11:5). Thus the image and likeness of God in Adam—divine sonship—is renewed with Seth and his family line (see Genesis 5).

Genesis 6 intimates, however, that the Sethite line is compromised through mixed marriages with the women of Cain's family. Seduced by their beauty, the Sethites (the "sons of God") enter into illicit unions with the Cainite women, "the daughters of men" (Genesis 6:2). The wicked fruit of these mixed marriages are men of great pride and extreme violence. They are called "the men of renown" (Genesis 6:4)—literally, "the men of the name (*shem*)." Here again *shem* refers to the pursuit of glory, but it is their own glory rather than God's. The offspring of these mixed marriages fall away from the covenant and embrace wickedness (see Genesis 6:5–6).

Saved Through Water

The wickedness of humanity reaches its pinnacle: "The LORD saw that the wickedness of man was great in the earth, and that every imagination of the thoughts of his heart was only evil continually" (Genesis 6:5). Further, "all flesh had corrupted their way," and "the earth [was] filled with violence" (Genesis 6:11, 12). Noah alone "walked with God" (Genesis 6:9).

This state of affairs provokes God to pronounce severe judgment. He chooses righteous Noah to serve as the covenant mediator between God and people. Thus Noah and his household form a righteous remnant through whom God will bring about a new beginning. God instructs Noah to build the ark in order to save his family as well as representatives of every beast and bird.

Noah responds in obedience. By faith "Noah did…all that God commanded him" (Genesis 6:22; see Hebrews 11:7). Noah bears witness to a wicked generation of God's impending judgment (the Flood) and his covenant mercy (the ark).

A New Creation. The Hebrew word for covenant, *berith* [beh-reet´], is first used in Genesis 6:18: "I will establish my covenant with you; and you shall come into the ark, you, your sons, your wife, and your sons' wives with you." The Hebrew statement that God will establish his covenant implies a *renewal* of a previous covenant. Thus God is not doing something radically new or different; he is promising to renew the covenant of Creation. He wants to renew his covenant with Noah's household.

There are several significant parallels between the Flood narrative (see Genesis 6—8) and the Creation account (see Genesis 1—2). In both narratives a new world emerges from the waters of "the deep" (see Genesis 1:2; 7:11). The number seven recurs in both accounts: Noah and his family board the ark and wait *seven* days before the Flood begins (see Genesis 7:10); the ark rests in the *seventh* month (see Genesis 8:4); Noah sends out birds every *seven* days (see Genesis 8:10–12); Noah takes *seven* pairs of "clean animals" (animals acceptable for sacrifice) into the ark (see Genesis 7:2).

Additionally, Noah's name means "rest" or "relief" (see Genesis 5:29), reflecting the seventh-day Sabbath mandate. The Sabbath is the sign of God's covenant with creation; the rainbow becomes the sign of God's renewed covenant with creation.

In the last lesson we saw how God established a covenant with Adam as *husband*. In this lesson we see how God renews his covenant with Noah as *husband*. Even more than husband, however, God renews his covenant with Noah as *father of a household*. There are four marriages on the ark, and Noah is head of the covenant family.

A New Adam. Thus God renews his covenant with Noah, his family and all creation through sacrifice and worship (see Genesis 8:20–22; 9:8, 17). He is called to "re-found" God's covenant family, like a new Adam. Just as there are parallels between the Flood and Creation, so there are significant parallels between Noah and Adam.

Like Adam, Noah is told to "be fruitful and multiply, and fill the earth" (Genesis 1:28; 9:1). Like Adam, Noah is given dominion over the creatures of the earth (see Genesis 1:28; 9:2). Both Adam and Noah find themselves in a garden or vineyard (see Genesis 2:15; 9:20). Both Adam and Noah consume fruit that exposes their nakedness (see Genesis 3:6–7; 9:21). And even after the Fall, both still bear the image of God (see Genesis 1:26; 9:6).

God's covenant with Noah renews divine sonship, restores royal dominion and resumes priestly sacrifice. But just as Adam's family divided into godly and ungodly lines, so does Noah's family.

The Table of Nations

Genesis 10 contains Noah's genealogy, identifying seventy descendants who founded the nations of the ancient world. This "table of nations" is absolutely unique: No other ancient genealogy portrays the entire human race as one worldwide family. It reveals God's fatherly perspective and purpose for humanity. It shows how the original unity of the human family in Adam is restored in Noah. It also demonstrates the ongoing pattern of human sin and divine judgment.

The table of nations helps the people of God understand their place in the world. It shows the righteous line, the descendents of Shem and Eber, who they are: bearers of God's blessing to the human race.

Through Noah's faithful firstborn son, Shem, God continues to build his covenant family. As we have seen, *shem* is also the word used for "name"—the term for "glory" and "fame." While the wicked pursue their own vainglory, Shem's righteous line seeks to advance the glory of God.

Ancient Israel traces its national origin back to the righteous descendants of Noah who bear the blessing: Shem and Eber. Shem's ancestors are called "Semites." Eber (from whom we get the word *Hebrew*) is the great-grandson of Shem. The children of Eber are the ancestors of Abraham, Isaac and Israel (see Genesis 11:10–26).

Conversely, the unrighteous line of Ham is the source of moral corruption and conflict. In fact, the rest of Old Testament history records the ongoing suffering of Israel at the hands of Ham's wicked descendants. Ham's line reads like a Who's Who list of Israel's enemies: Egyptians, Canaanities, Philistines, Assyrians and Babylonians (see Genesis 10:6–20).[1]

The Tower of Babel. The conflict between the lines of Shem and Ham first surfaces during the building of the Tower of Babel in Genesis 11. The wicked people of the earth know that God once destroyed the earth with a flood. And like the people of that time, the descendants of Noah fall into sin and bring down God's judgment.

They begin construction of a tower, an ancient temple, wishing to establish their own fame. They want to make a *shem* for themselves (see Genesis 11:4). They oppose the line of the righteous son, Shem. (Notice how this story is placed in between two genealogies of Shem, Genesis 10:21–32 and 11:10–32.)

The *Catechism* states that through the "perversion of paganism," fallen humanity is "united only in its perverse ambition to forge its own unity as at

Babel (Cf. *Wis* 10:5; *Gen* 11:4-6)." It states that the ungodly commit the sins of "polytheism and the idolatry of the nation and of its rulers" (*CCC*, 57).

At Babel God again brings judgment, this time confusing the people's language. They are scattered to the four corners of the earth.

God's covenant with Noah is far-reaching. Though sin shatters the human race into separate peoples, God extends his providential care to the nations. He extends his covenant with Noah to "all flesh that is upon the earth" (Genesis 9:17). "The covenant with Noah remains in force during the times of the Gentiles, until the universal proclamation of the Gospel (Cf. *Gen* 9:13; *Lk* 21:24; *DV* 3)" (*CCC*, 58).

A Flood of Comparisons.   The covenant with Noah points us to the sacrament of baptism (see 1 Peter 3:20–21). The Flood is a type of baptism. Like the Flood, baptism cleanses us and destroys sin. Furthermore, as a kind of new creation appeared through the waters of destruction, so those who are baptized are new creations in Christ.

We also receive a similar warning: Just as Noah's son Ham was saved on the ark but did evil and received a curse instead of a blessing, so baptism places us in a state of grace that needs to be maintained (see *CCC*, 701, 1219, 1269). As in the days of Noah, many in the world today have rejected the Lord. We need to devote ourselves to our sacrificial worship, as Noah and the righteous line of Seth did.

The Literary Framework of Genesis 1—11

At first glance the multiple genealogies in Genesis may seem like superfluous information. However, a closer look at these sections reveals the literary artistry of Genesis.

The various stories of Genesis are connected through the use of the Hebrew word for "generations," *toledoth* [to´ leh dote]. Genesis 2:4 introduces the history of the human family by saying, "These are the generations (*toledoth*) of the heavens and the earth." The same term advances the story through the lines of Noah and the patriarchs: "This is the book of the generations of Adam" (Genesis 5:1); and, "These are the generations of Noah" (Genesis 6:9).

The repetition of *generations* points to a deliberate literary framework. The term is used *ten times* in Genesis to introduce key figures in salvation history. It reveals the narrative plot of the history of God's family. History is not just about wars, politics and economics; it is the story of the human race as the family of God.

The author of Genesis links Adam and Eve to Noah, Abraham and the rest of salvation history. We see this literary structure in the first eleven chapters of Genesis. It reveals that salvation history is shaped by spiritual conflict between the godly and the ungodly, that righteousness and wickedness travel down family lines and that God vindicates his family and judges those who corrupt it.

From Adam to Noah there are ten generations (see Genesis 5). The wicked of these generations can trace their lineage back to Cain. At the end of the ten generations, God sends judgment on the world in the form of a flood.

Noah has three sons: Shem, Japheth and Ham. Shem receives the blessing of the firstborn. Ham's descendant Canaan brings forth the wicked of the post-Flood world. From Shem to Terah there are ten generations. Then God sends

The Literary Framework of Genesis 1–11

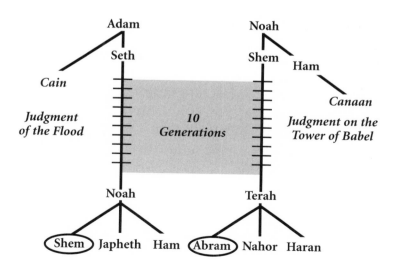

judgment on the Tower of Babel. Terah has three sons: Abram, Nahor and Haran. Abram receives the blessing from God.

In the past two lessons we have looked at the conflict within the human family, a conflict between two *seeds* (see Genesis 3:15), two *sons* (see Genesis 4–5; 10) and two *lines* (the *righteous* and the *unrighteous*). In his famous work *The City of God,* Saint Augustine understood Genesis in terms of two cities: the City of God, which is based upon the love of God even to the point of the contempt of self, and the City of Man, which is based upon the love of self even to the point of the contempt of God. Certainly we find ourselves facing a challenge: How do we live as citizens of the City of God while sojourning in the City of Man?

Review Questions for Personal Study

1. How is the story of Noah and the Flood like the Creation account?

2. How does the Flood prefigure baptism?

3. How does Christ fulfill the Creation covenant?

4. Describe the parallel structure of Genesis 1—11 in terms of *toledoth*.

Recommended Verses to Memorize

Genesis 6:5

Hebrews 11:1

1 Peter 3:21

Abraham: Our Father in Faith

This fourth lesson focuses on God's covenant with Abraham and the connection between covenant blessing and trials for God's faithful people in the example of Abraham. God gives to Abraham the covenant blessing, and then through Abraham he gives it to all the nations. God rewards Abraham's obedience through covenant renewal, so that ultimately all those whom God has scattered because of the Tower of Babel can be regathered as the family of God.

We conclude with a brief history of the sojourn of the Hebrews in Egypt, leading up to the Exodus.

And God Blessed Them...

From the beginning God pronounced his blessing on creation (see Genesis 1:22, 28; 2:3). Life—both the gift of life itself and life-giving power ("be fruitful and multiply")—reveals God's blessing. The blessing of the covenant is given and received through the family. In fact, both natural life and covenant blessing are shared within the family and are part of the family legacy.

Genesis shows how the blessing passes from father to son. After the Flood God restores the blessing through Noah (see Genesis 9:1). Noah then blesses his firstborn son, Shem (see Genesis 9:26). Through Shem Noah's family receives God's blessing (see Genesis 9:27).

When humanity rejects God, attempting unity without God at the Tower of Babel, God scatters those who are in rebellion (see Genesis 11). Later he promises to bless Abraham for his obedience and through him restore humanity (see Genesis 12).

In Genesis 12:1–3 God uses the term *bless* or *blessing* five times. The divine blessing is transmitted through family lines (that is, Abraham's descendants). Furthermore, humanity will not be united through making a name for itself;

only through God will Abraham's name—his *shem*—be made great (see Genesis 12:2). Thus the covenant blessing passed on through Shem will now come through his descendant Abraham.

From Adam to Noah God expanded his family from two people to a family. Now God expands his family even further: whereas Noah was the *father* of a *household*, Abraham is the head of an extended family, the *chieftain* of a *tribe*.

Adam triggered the covenant curses through his disobedience; Abraham secures God's blessing through his righteousness. Thus in *Abraham* the failure of Adam is partially reversed, and through his *seed* God promises to bless all humanity again. In Genesis 12:1–3 God promises Abram three things: *land* and *nationhood* (see 12:1–2), a *dynastic kingdom* (see 12:2, "a great name") and a *worldwide family* (see 12:3). Eventually God strengthens Abraham's faith by upgrading his threefold promise with three covenant oaths (see Genesis 15, 17, 22). God swears these oaths to Abraham because of his patient endurance and faithfulness (see Hebrews 6:13–17).

Abraham Responds in Faith

When God calls Abram (meaning "exalted father"), he is seventy-five years old. Abram is extremely wealthy but has no heir (see Genesis 12:4–5; 13:2; 16:1). At God's command Abram leaves his home for a nomadic life with part of his clan: his wife Sarai, his nephew Lot and many domestic servants and their families (see Genesis 12:4–9). Abram is already demonstrating that he is a man of faith (see Hebrews 11:8)! Later, God renames him Abraham, which means "father of a multitude" (Genesis 17:4–5).

However, Abraham's life reveals that the road to blessing is paved with trials and temptations. He faces a multitude of hardships, including famine (see Genesis 12:10), exile and temporary "loss" of his wife (see Genesis 12:10–20; 20), family strife and division (see Genesis 13), wars (see Genesis 14:1–16), unfulfilled promises (see Genesis 15), marital discord (see Genesis 16), surgery (circumcision) (see Genesis 17), the supernatural destruction of Sodom and Gomorrah (see Genesis 18:16—19:29), more family strife and division (see Genesis 21:8–21) and the ultimate trial of a father, the offering of his beloved son (see Genesis 22:1–19).

Abraham grows in faith through these tests, and he makes ever greater sacrifices. In the midst of his trials, God fulfills his promise to bless him (see

Genesis 14:17–20). Abraham defeats his enemies; then he meets Melchizedek, whose name means "righteous king" of "Salem" (Hebrew for "peace"). More than just a king, Melchizedek is a *priest* of God Most High. (This is the first reference in Scripture to a priest.) Melchizedek offers bread and wine to Abram, and then he gives God's blessing to Abram. Abram's response is one of homage by paying him tithes. In short, Melchizedek prefigures Christ in three ways: (1) he is a priest-king who (2) offers bread and wine and (3) receives homage.

Three Promises Strengthened by Three Oaths

In Genesis 12 God makes three promises to Abram: *a nation with its own land* (see Genesis 12:2), *kingship* (a great name, a royal dynasty) (see Genesis 12:2) and *worldwide blessing* (see Genesis 12:3). God rewards Abram's faith with three covenant *oaths* recorded in Genesis 15, 17 and 22.

The First Covenant Oath. In Genesis 15 Abram is still childless. When God promises him a great reward (see verse 1), Abram respectfully reminds God, *what good is a reward if he has no son to inherit it?* In response God swears a covenant oath to give Abram a son. God makes a covenant with him when God passes between the parts of animals cut in two by Abram (see 15:7–21).

The first blessing that God promised Abram in Genesis 12:2, land and nationhood, is upgraded to a covenant oath. God swears that Abram will be a father to innumerable descendants, who will be delivered from bondage and receive the Promised Land (see Genesis 15:13–16). This foreshadows not only the Hebrews' slavery but also their exodus from Egypt.

As time goes by, however, elderly Abram and his wife, Sarai, grow impatient. They decide to take matters into their own hands. Sarai tells Abram that he should take her Egyptian handmaid, Hagar, and have a son through her (see Genesis 16:1–3). Abram complies. However, after Hagar conceives a son, she begins to look at Sarai with contempt, sowing seeds of family discord (see Genesis 16:4).

The Second Covenant Oath. At this point God renames Abram "Abraham," meaning "father of a multitude" (Genesis 17:5). He also renames Sarai "Sarah," meaning "great mother" (Genesis 17:15). God swears another covenant oath to Abraham to give him a son through his wife Sarah; Ishmael is *not* the chosen heir. God gives an amazing promise: not just descendants but "kings of peoples shall come from [Sarah]" (Genesis 17:16). This prefigures the covenant God will make with David to establish his kingdom in 2 Samuel 7:9.

God promises that Abraham will have a son in one year through Sarah (see Genesis 17:21). The promise includes a command, however: Abraham must circumcise himself and all the males in his tribe (see Genesis 17:10–14). Ishmael is thirteen years old and is circumcised, as are the household slaves. From this day forth all descendants of Abraham shall be circumcised on the eighth day.

At this point Abraham is ninety-nine years old. He has three months to recover and conceive with his wife Sarah! Even in his obedience to be circumcised Abraham demonstrates great faith.

Just as God promised, Isaac is born one year later. After he is weaned Abraham has a great feast (see Genesis 21:8). Fearful that Ishmael may try to usurp Isaac, Sarah asks Abraham to banish Hagar and Ishmael once and for all from their midst (see Genesis 21:10). Abraham hesitates, until the Lord instructs him to do as Sarah requests.

The Final Covenant Oath.　Once Ishmael is banished, Abraham is left with his only beloved son Isaac. Years pass before God gives Abraham the ultimate test: He asks Abraham to sacrifice his son on a mountain of Moriah (see Genesis 22:1–2).

Abraham obeys immediately. He prepares the supplies himself, and he sets off with Isaac on the three-day journey (see Genesis 22:3–4). Once they arrive at the appointed place, Isaac carries the wood of the sacrifice up the hill (see Genesis 22:6). When he asks his father, "Where is the lamb for the burnt offering?" Abraham responds, "God will provide himself the lamb" (Genesis 22:7–8).

Abraham binds Isaac and lays him upon the altar. Just as Abraham is about to plunge the knife into his beloved son, the Lord commands Abraham to spare Isaac. Abraham spots a ram, and he offers it to the Lord instead of his son. For the third and final time, God renews his covenant with Abraham, and he swears to bless all of the nations through the seed of Abraham (see Genesis 22:11–18).

This is similar to God's promise in Genesis 3, where he promises to bring deliverance through the "seed" of the woman (Genesis 3:15). Now God promises to save the world through the "seed" of Abraham. Ultimately woman did not bring salvation to the world: it was her "seed"—the Christ—who became man and was born of a woman. Likewise, salvation will not come through Abraham but through his seed, who is also Christ (see Matthew 1:1).

All of humanity is cursed through the disobedience of Adam. However, all of humanity is blessed through Abraham's obedience. Abraham obeys God by offering his only beloved son. In Abraham the curse of the Fall is partially reversed; through Abraham's "seed," Christ, the curse will be fully reversed.

Three Oaths. In Genesis 15 God promises that Abram's descendants will be delivered from bondage in a foreign nation and will be given the Promised Land (see Genesis 15:13–14). In Genesis 17 God promises that kings will come forth from Abraham and Sarah (see verse 6). And in Genesis 22 God declares that all nations will be blessed through Abraham's descendants (see verse 18).

These three covenant oaths will be fulfilled by the *Exodus* and the *Mosaic covenant*, the *kingdom* and the *Davidic covenant*, and *Jesus Christ* and the *new covenant*.

The Obedience of Abraham and Isaac

Abraham is not the only person who has faith in God; Isaac's obedience is also implied in the biblical narrative. The ancient rabbis called this story the *aqedah* [ah´ kuh duh]—the "binding"—of Isaac (Genesis 22:9). This story is as much about Isaac's self-offering as it is about Abraham's faithfulness. Isaac is a grown youth, strong enough to carry the wood up the mountain (see Genensis 22:6) and thus easily capable of overcoming his elderly father. Therefore, Jewish tradition holds that Isaac asked to be bound so that he would not struggle against his father when he was being sacrificed.

The early Church fathers understood this story as a foreshadowing of the sacrifice of Jesus. Like Isaac, Jesus is the only beloved Son of the Father who is sacrificed for the salvation of the world (see Genesis 22:2; John 3:16; Romans 8:32). Like Isaac, Jesus fully submits to his Father's will and carries the wood up the mountain (see Genesis 22:6; John 19:17). Hebrews 11:19 tells us that Abraham was willing to sacrifice his son because he "considered that God was able to raise men even from the dead." Jesus rises from the dead on the third day, just as Abraham received his son back from the sentence of death on the third day (see Genesis 22:4; 1 Corinthians 15:4).

In the Church's liturgy Genesis 22 is read in connection with Jesus' transfiguration. It is during the Transfiguration that the apostles hear God the Father say, "This is my beloved Son" (Mark 9:7). This evokes God's word to Abraham:

"Take your son, your only-begotten son Isaac, whom you love, and go to the land of Moriah, and offer him there as a burnt offering upon one of the mountains of which I shall tell you" (Genesis 22:2). The difference, of course, is that God the Father does not stop the death of his beloved Son but lets Jesus' self-offering fulfill all of the covenants.

Little does Abraham know that his actions foreshadow how God will bring about the blessing of all the nations. In Christ Abraham's words come true: "God will provide himself the lamb" (Genesis 22:8). Mount Moriah, the place where Abraham offers Isaac, is part of a chain of mountains outside Jerusalem. Later in Israel's history the temple of Jerusalem is built on Mount Moriah (see 2 Chronicles 3:1). There the people of Israel offer their sacrifices—in effect reminding God of his covenant promise to Abraham—until the need for these sacrifices ends when Christ comes as the true Lamb of God. Indeed, Calvary—the place where Jesus is crucified—is one of the peaks of Moriah.

A Scriptural Pattern: The Elder Serves the Younger

According to how the world thinks, an elder son is stronger than a younger son and has "firstborn" privileges. Often this very situation is the downfall of the elder. Over and over again in Scripture, the older son is prideful. Adam, the "firstborn" of creation, falls into pride. Cain, the elder brother, kills his righteous younger brother.

Abraham's son Isaac has two sons, Esau and Jacob. But just as God chose Abraham's younger son (Isaac) over his elder son (Ishmael), so Jacob is chosen over Esau (see Genesis 27). This is a subplot that runs throughout the Bible: The younger is chosen over the elder.

God chooses the weaker, younger brother to show that his plans are fulfilled through *his* power, not that of men. Later God preserves Joseph after his older brothers sell him into slavery (see Genesis 37, 39—47). Much later King David is chosen over his numerous older brothers (see 1 Samuel 16:13).

Saint Paul explains: God chooses the younger brother over the older "in order that God's purpose of election might continue, not because of works but because of his call.… So it depends not upon man's will or exertion, but upon God's mercy" (Romans 9:11, 16).

Into Egypt

Just as Abram is renamed Abraham, so Isaac's son Jacob is later renamed Israel. Israel has twelve sons, and they become the fathers of the twelve tribes of the nation of Israel.

The Book of Genesis ends with the familiar story of Joseph. Jacob (or Israel) gives his son Joseph a special coat, and out of jealousy his brothers sell him into slavery. As a slave in Egypt, Joseph receives from the Lord the ability to interpret dreams. Joseph's use of this gift saves the Egyptians and many others from famine. As a result Joseph becomes prime minister of Egypt (see Genesis 41:39–40).

Joseph is reunited with his brothers when they come to Egypt during the famine to buy food. Instead of returning to the land God has given Abraham, Joseph's family remains in Egypt, where they live on the choicest land under his protection. Centuries later a new Pharaoh arises who sees the Hebrews as a threat.

The sons of Israel become enslaved, as God told Abraham would happen. They cry to God for help, and he raises up a deliverer, fulfilling his promises to Joseph—"God will be with you, and will bring you again to the land of your fathers" (Genesis 48:21)—and to Abraham that his descendants would be delivered from slavery (see Genesis 15:13–14). We will study this deliverer, Moses, in the next lesson.

Review Questions for Personal Study

1. What are the three promises God makes to Abraham in Genesis 12:1–3?

2. How do the three promises relate to the covenant oaths God swears in Genesis 15, 17 and 22?

3. What is the relationship of these covenant promises to future events in salvation history?

4. Read Hebrews 6:19—7:2. How does Melchizedek foreshadow Christ?

5. How does Abraham's offering of his beloved son Isaac help us understand God the Father's offering of Jesus for the atonement for our sins?

6. What can we learn from Abraham's example of total surrender?

7. How does the phrase "the elder shall serve the younger" describe a sub-plot of Scripture?

Recommended Verses to Memorize

Genesis 12:1–3

John 3:16

Moses and the Israelites

There was a person named Israel *before* there was a nation called Israel. (The nation is named after the man.) Abraham was the father of Isaac, and Isaac was the father of Jacob. Jacob was renamed Israel (see Genesis 35:10). Israel had twelve sons, and these twelve sons became the fathers of twelve tribes, the twelve tribes of Israel. Then tragedy struck: These twelve tribes became slaves in Egypt.

God's Firstborn Son

Genesis reveals that salvation history is the story of God's family. God creates Adam as his firstborn son of creation. Though Adam sins, God the Father does not give up on humanity. God promises to restore humanity through Abraham.

The families in Genesis become nations. God calls Abraham's descendants—the nation of Israel—to be his "firstborn son" among the nations. Tragically, like Adam, Israel fails to realize its calling to be a faithful firstborn son. All is not lost, however: God stoops down to Israel's level as a good father, hoping to raise the nation from its sin to a restored relationship with him.

In Genesis God warns Abraham that his descendants will end up in slavery; however, he promises to deliver them from bondage and return them to the Promised Land (see Genesis 15:13–16, 18). Exodus tells us how God fulfills his covenant promises.

Although Israel is in servitude in Egypt, God wants to do more than just give the nation *political liberation*. The Scriptures show us that the Israelites were actually in the worst kind of bondage: They were in *spiritual* bondage! The Book of Ezekiel tells us that the Israelites begin worshiping the gods of Egypt before the Exodus (see Ezekiel 20:6–9). Thus, the goal of the Exodus is more than political independence: It is to call Israel out of Egypt to worship the Lord. God tells Moses to say on his behalf to Pharaoh, "Let my people go, that they may serve me in the wilderness" (Exodus 7:16). God wants to deliver Israel from serving and worshiping the gods of Egypt so that they can serve and worship him, the *true* God!

The Call of Moses

Fearing the growing Hebrew population, Pharaoh orders the slaughter of all the male Hebrew children (see Exodus 1:8, 15–22). One mother is able to save her child from death by placing him in a basket in the reeds at the edge of the Nile River. One of Pharaoh's daughters finds the child in the water, and she takes him into her home and raises him as her own son. She names the child "Moses," which means "taken from water" (Exodus 2:1–10).

Forty years later Moses sees an Egyptian taskmaster beating one of his fellow Hebrews. Moses intervenes and kills the taskmaster. Then he has to flee into the desert, a wanted man. He eventually settles down with a Midianite family and becomes a shepherd (see Exodus 2:11–25).

Forty years later, while he is tending his flock one day, Moses spots a burning bush whose flames seem inextinguishable. When he approaches the bush, God calls to him. The Lord identifies himself as the God of Abraham, Isaac and Jacob. He tells Moses that he has heard the cry of his enslaved people, and he promises to deliver them and bring them to the Promised Land (see Exodus 3:2, 6–8).

God relates his plan to Moses: Moses is to ask Pharaoh to let Israel go on a three-day journey into the wilderness to sacrifice to the Lord. God tells Moses that Pharaoh will harden his heart and refuse Moses' request. Because of this, God will bring judgment on the Egyptians. He will lead the Israelites out of bondage and bring them into the Promised Land (see Exodus 3:18–20).

God calls Israel his "firstborn son" among the nations. When Pharaoh refuses to release God's firstborn son, the Lord will slay Pharaoh's firstborn son (see Exodus 4:22–23).

Deliverance From Egypt

Many people wonder why God asks the Israelites to sacrifice animals like cattle, sheep and goats. It is not because God enjoys the smell of burning meat.

Moses explains to Pharaoh why the Israelites must be allowed to go out to the desert to offer their sacrifices to the Lord: Their sacrifices would be "abominable" to the Egyptians (see Exodus 8:25–27). What is so offensive about Israel's sacrifices?

Israel is to sacrifice to God the very animals that the Egyptians worship as gods. God wants Israel to renounce the gods of Egypt and to worship him as the one true God. God wants them to serve him and *only* him!

When Pharaoh refuses to let the people go, God responds by sending ten famous plagues to Egypt. These plagues symbolize judgment on the gods of Egypt. Here are a few examples: In turning the Nile to blood, God symbolizes his victory over the Egyptian god Hapi, who governs the Nile (see Exodus 7:14–25). With the plague of frogs, the frog goddess Heket is mocked (see Exodus 8:1–15). The bull gods Apis and Hathor are judged in the destruction of cattle (see Exodus 9:1–7). With the plague of darkness, the sun god Re is defeated (see Exodus 10:21–23).

Even after nine plagues, however, Pharaoh still refuses to release God's first-born son, Israel. Because of this insubordination, God threatens the firstborn sons of the Egyptians. The Lord tells Moses that he will send his angel of death to slay the firstborn sons in Egypt and the firstborn male offspring of all live-stock (see Exodus 11:4–9). And God gives Israel a way to save their firstborn sons: the Passover (see Exodus 12:1–27).

The Israelites are instructed to *sacrifice* unblemished lambs, *spread* the blood over their doorposts and *eat* the lambs as part of a sacred meal (see Exodus 12:5–11). By slaying these animals God symbolically slaughters the gods of Egypt: "On all the gods of Egypt I will execute judgment" (Exodus 12:12). All of the Israelites who obey are "passed over," and their firstborn sons are spared (see Exodus 12:13).

The death of his firstborn son is the event that finally breaks Pharaoh (see Exodus 12:30–32), and he drives the people of Israel out of the land. God appears before Israel as a pillar of cloud by day and a pillar of fire by night. He leads his people out of Egypt and through the Red Sea (see Exodus 13:21; see 14—15).

Even when the Israelites doubt God and complain against him, the Lord cares for his people. The people grow weary of the difficult journey, and they begin to grumble against Moses and the Lord. They complain that they are *hungry*, and the Lord sends miraculous bread from heaven to feed them (see Exodus 16). Then they protest that there is no *water*, so the Lord gives them miraculous water from a rock (see Exodus 17).

Saint Paul explains that this foreshadows the new covenant: Just as the Holy Spirit led Israel through the Red Sea under Moses, so we are baptized into Christ and the Spirit in the baptismal waters. Furthermore, Moses gave the people heavenly bread and supernatural drink; Jesus gives us the Eucharist (see 1 Corinthians 10:1–4).

When the Israelites enter the desert, their major issue is trust: Will the people trust God to provide for their needs? Will they be content with God's provision (see Genesis 22:8, 14)? Or will they murmur against God, assuming he will not provide?

The First Covenant With Israel

The Lord brings his people to Mount Sinai. Here he declares they are a "kingdom of priests and a holy nation" (Exodus 19:6). He gives Israel the Ten Commandments (see Exodus 20:1–17; 32:16). In addition he gives them civil laws, telling them how to deal with certain criminal actions (see Exodus 21—23).

Moses builds an altar with twelve pillars, symbolizing that all twelve tribes will enter into the covenant. Then Israel offers sacrifice to God. The people swear: "All that the LORD has spoken we will do, and we will be obedient" (Exodus 24:7; see also verse 3). Moses calls the blood of the sacrificed animals "the blood of the covenant which the LORD has made with you" (Exodus 24:8). The covenant is ratified with a meal when Moses and the elders eat in the presence of God (see Exodus 24:9–11).

God's covenant directions climax when Moses ascends the mountain of the Lord and stays there for forty days and forty nights (see Exodus 24:15–18). There he receives a vision of a heavenly pattern for the tent of worship, the mobile temple (see Exodus 25:9). Ancient Israelites understood this to mean that Moses saw the heavenly temple, of which the earthly tent and temple were a copy. The Book of Hebrews tells us that those who serve in the earthly temple "serve a copy and shadow of the heavenly sanctuary" (Hebrews 8:5).

The prophets also have visions of the heavenly temple. Isaiah is caught up to the heavenly throne room, where he sees the cherubim before the Lord (see Isaiah 6). It is the apostle John, however, who provides the fullest description of the heavenly Jerusalem in the Apocalypse (see Revelation 21—22). He says, "I saw no temple in the city, for its temple is the Lord God the Almighty and the Lamb" (Revelation 21:22).

We see that God's purpose in delivering Israel was to give them his *law* and to bring them into his presence through *worship*. God wants to teach Israel and to have them enter into communion with him.

God's Second Covenant With Israel

Tragically, while Moses is up on the mountain, Israel reverts to the idolatrous practices of the Egyptians. The people construct an image of the Egyptian god Apis, a bull god (see Exodus 32:1–6). Though God brings Israel out of Egypt, taking Egypt out of Israel proves more difficult.

In worshiping the golden calf, Israel succumbs to three major temptations: money, sex and power. First, the people surrender to the idol of *wealth* by worshiping the *golden* calf. Second, the worship of Apis involves *sexual immorality* (see Exodus 32:6, 25). Finally, the bull-god represents *virility, power* and *strength*.

When Israel breaks the covenant, the nation deserves the covenant curse of death. Speaking to Moses, God does not refer to Israel as "*my* people" but as "*your* people, whom *you* brought up out of the land of Egypt" (Exodus 32:7; see 3:10, 5:1, 6:7). God tells Moses, "Let me alone, that my wrath may burn hot against them and I may consume them" (Exodus 32:10).

Moses, however, reminds God of his oath to Abraham. If God destroys the Israelites, he will be killing Abraham's chosen descendants. That would break his promise to bless all the nations through them (see Exodus 32:13).

God has not forgotten his oath. He wants Moses to realize why he swore it to Abraham: He knew that Israel would need it! God programmed the covenant with merciful provisions that he knew the people would need.

Moses comes down from the mountain and, upon seeing the idolatry of Israel, smashes the tablets of the Ten Commandments (see Exodus 32:15–19). This symbolizes what Israel has done: The people have broken their covenant with the Lord. Then Moses shouts, "Who is on the Lord's side?"

The Levites respond, and Moses instructs them to kill the idolaters. Three thousand Israelites die because of their idolatry that day (see Exodus 32:26–28). Moses then tells the Levites, "Today you have ordained yourselves for the service of the LORD, each one at the cost of his son and of his brother, that he may bestow a blessing upon you this day" (Exodus 32:29).

Now the covenant law changes. Israel has revealed its spiritual bondage to the gods of Egypt. To help purify the people of their idolatrous tendencies, God gives Moses an elaborate code of ritual purity laws, recounted in the Book of Leviticus. These laws are designed, in part, to quarantine Israel from the gentiles and their practices. These purity laws imply that Israel is not yet holy enough to go out and evangelize the nations. The people must first learn humility.

Moreover, God gives exhaustive instructions for continual animal sacrifice. Since the Israelites worshiped a golden calf, they must regularly sacrifice calves, sheep and goats, renouncing the gods of Egypt.

Prior to their sin Israel was called "a kingdom of priests" (Exodus 19:6). Now the Levites alone shall serve as priests. Thus the Book of Leviticus explains to the Levites the purity laws of the priests (see Leviticus 1—16) and the laws they are to teach the people to make them holy (see Leviticus 17—26).

Rebellions and Rules

The Israelites continue to rebel. The Book of Numbers presents a pattern throughout its pages: Israel sins, and God gives Israel more laws. The laws are a means to teach Israel to acknowledge her weakness and turn to the Lord (see Galatians 3:19).

When the Israelites finally arrive at the border of the land promised to them, they refuse to enter into it. They fear those who inhabit the land, even though the Lord has promised them the land and victory over those who dwell in it (see Numbers 13:30—14:10).

By rejecting the Lord, the Israelites prove that they are beyond rehabilitation. The Lord promises that the current generation—except for Joshua and Caleb— will never enter the land. They will wander the desert until they die. The Lord will bring the next generation into the land (see Numbers 14:20–35).

Sadly, however, forty years later the next generation proves to be no less wicked. They fall into the same sin of idolatry, just as their fathers did before them, to Ba'al at Peor (see Numbers 25).

Deuteronomy means "second law"; due to their sinfulness God gives Israel a "lower law." Deuteronomy, therefore, is not promulgated in the words of God but in the words of Moses. The book makes concessions, such as permitting divorce and genocidal warfare, that are absent in previous covenant legislations. According to Jesus, Moses gives these lower laws to Israel due to the hardness of their heart (see Ezekiel 20:25; Matthew 19:8).

The fathers of the Church recognized this "divine condescension" as an example of how our heavenly Father stoops down to the level of his children. Saint Paul calls the Law "our custodian until Christ came, that we might be justified by faith" (Galatians 3:24). The Deuteronomic Law was meant to teach Israel how to "grow up" in holiness. When Christ comes, however, these Deuteronomic law codes are no longer necessary. "Now that faith has come, we are no longer under a custodian" (Galatians 3:25).

The Book of Deuteronomy also recounts the instructions that Moses gives Israel for reconquering the land promised to Abraham, Isaac and Jacob. The conditions of the Deuteronomic covenant will be fulfilled when the Lord gives Israel "rest from all your enemies round about" (Deuteronomy 12:10). At that time the Lord will show Israel where they are to build the temple (see Deuteronomy 12:11). In other words, the goal of Deuteronomy, just like the Book of Exodus, concerns liturgy and worship, not just political independence. God wants Israel to worship him, and once the instructions of Deuteronomy are fulfilled, the nation will worship in a temple.

Jesus as the New Moses

The person and work of Jesus is foreshadowed in Moses and the events of Israel's Passover and Exodus. Like Moses, Jesus is born during the reign of a ruthless king who kills other Hebrew male children. Like Israel, Jesus sojourns in Egypt and is called back to his birthplace after a period of exile. He passes through waters—his baptism in the Jordan—and goes out into the wilderness, where he is tested by a forty-day fast.

Jesus' first miracle is turning water into wine, and he later turns wine into blood, recalling the first plague of Exodus. He teaches from a mountain, just as Moses' teaching issued from his visitation on a mountain. Jesus' appearance on a mountain before three companions radiates God's glory, just as Moses' face shone on his descent from the mountain after speaking with God (see Exodus 34:29–35). Jesus gives heavenly bread and spiritual drink to God's people (the Eucharist), as foreshadowed by the manna in the desert. He appoints a set of twelve leaders (the apostles) and then an additional set of seventy disciples, just as Moses appointed judges to help him govern Israel in the desert (see Matthew 10:1; Exodus 18:13–24). Jesus is the true Passover Lamb, and he leads us out of spiritual bondage in the New Exodus.

Thus God uses the historical events in the Old Testament to prefigure the salvation Christ brings in the New. Through Israel's Passover God delivers the nation from the bondage of slavery and leads them to the Promised Land. In the New Passover Christ delivers us from the bondage of sin and leads us to the heavenly Jerusalem, the true Promised Land.

Furthermore, Israel's Passover prefigures the paschal mystery of the new covenant. In Israel's Passover a lamb is sacrificed, its blood is shed, and it is eaten as part of a family meal. In the true Passover Christ is offered as the sacrificial Lamb of God; his blood is shed for the salvation of the world. Just as the Israelites had to eat the lamb, so the Church feeds upon the Body and Blood of Christ in the Eucharist. The Lamb has been sacrificed; now we must partake of the meal (see 1 Corinthians 5:7–8). In fact, Christ's words at the Last Supper evoke the covenant ratification ceremony at Sinai (see Matthew 26:27; Exodus 24:1–8).

So far we've seen how God has expanded his covenant family from a marriage, to a household, to a tribe, to twelve tribes. Under Moses God's covenant people have grown into a nation. In the next lesson we will see the climax of God's Old Testament plan: the kingdom.

Review Questions for Personal Study

1. How does the Book of Exodus show us that the Israelites were in not only political but also spiritual bondage?

2. In what way does the Book of Exodus show us God's judgment on the gods of the Egyptians?

3. Why did God instruct Israel to offer animal sacrifices?

4. How are God's instructions for regular animal sacrifice related to the first question above?

5. What was the goal of the Exodus?

6. How does Moses prefigure the person and work of Christ?

7. How is the Eucharist the New Passover?

Recommended Verses to Memorize

1 Corinthians 5:7–8

The Covenant With David

In this lesson we move to the fulfillment of the third covenant oath: the establishment of a kingdom through Abraham's line.

Into the Promised Land

Moses leads the people of Israel out of Egypt to Mount Sinai, where they make—and then break—the covenant (see Exodus 19, 32). Shortly thereafter they reject God's call to enter the Promised Land, and they are condemned to wander in the desert for forty years until the entire adult generation (except for Caleb and Joshua) dies (see Numbers 14:20–35).

After Moses dies Joshua finally brings the people into the land that was promised to Abraham, Isaac and Jacob-Israel (see Joshua 3—4). Joshua leads Israel in a series of battles to take back the land from the wicked people who took it while the Israelites were slaves in Egypt (see Joshua 6; 8–12). After they reclaim their land, Joshua allots portions to each tribe (see Joshua 13–21). He also renews the Deuteronomic covenant with Israel at Shechem (see Joshua 24:14–27).

Israel fights for generations against the Canaanites under certain men and women—called judges—whom God raises up to lead the people in a series of victories. Throughout the time of the judges, there is a three-D cycle: 1) *Disobedience*: one or more tribes become complacent about covenant faithfulness; 2) *Defeat*: God allows an enemy to humble the Israelites through defeat and servitude; 3) *Deliverance*: the Israelites cry out to God for help, and he sends a judge to deliver them and govern them in peace for a time. This cycle repeats many times.

Saul, the First King

Samuel—the last of the judges, a priest and a prophet—wants his sons to take his place, but the elders of Israel say it's time for a change: They want Samuel to appoint a king so they can be governed as are the nations nearby (see 1 Samuel 8:1–5). Samuel anoints Saul as the first king of Israel (see 1 Samuel 10:1). God exalts the humble when he chooses Saul from the smallest tribe, the tribe of Benjamin—the tribe of the youngest brother of the twelve sons of Israel (see 1 Samuel 9:21).

Saul, however, falls into error. First, rather than waiting for the prophet Samuel to offer sacrifice before a major battle, Saul presumes to offer the sacrifice himself. Samuel lets him know that this act of disobedience will cost him the dynasty. His sons will not succeed him as king (see 1 Samuel 13:8–14).

Second, Saul disobeys God's direct order to "strike Amalek, and utterly destroy all that they have" (1 Samuel 15:3). In the battle against the Amalekites, Saul spares their king and saves the best animals from the slaughter, with the pretext that the people will sacrifice these animals to the Lord (see 1 Samuel 15:8–9, 15). God's will must be done God's way, however; he desires obedience more than sacrifices (see 1 Samuel 15:22; Psalm 51:17). Saul's presumption costs him the kingdom. Shortly thereafter the Spirit of God departs from him, and he is plagued with an evil spirit (see 1 Samuel 15:26; 16:14).

David's Rise to Power

Without telling Saul, Samuel goes to the house of Jesse in Bethlehem, where he anoints David (the youngest of eight sons) as the second king of Israel (see 1 Samuel 16:11–13). David is a man after God's own heart (see 1 Samuel 13:14). For the honor of God's name, he defeats the Philistine champion Goliath with a slingshot (see 1 Samuel 17). He subsequently becomes a part of Saul's household, soothing Saul during his fits by playing music on a lyre. Saul doesn't know that this is the future king—filled with God's Spirit—who is calming him.

David's friendship with Jonathan, Saul's son, is unique. Jonathan knows that David will take his father's place, but he is at peace with God's plan (see 1 Samuel 20). However, when Saul realizes that David is God's anointed one, he tries to hunt David down to kill him. David, out of respect for Saul's office, does not kill Saul even when he has an opportunity to do so. Later on, when King Saul and his sons perish (see 1 Samuel 31), David laments over Saul and Jonathan (see 2 Samuel 1). He also offers a permanent place in his home and at his table for Saul's only living grandson, Mephibosheth (see 2 Samuel 9).

David conquers the last stronghold of the Canaanites, the famous city of

Jerusalem (see 2 Samuel 4:6–10). Here God desires to dwell in the midst of his people, now that they have defeated their enemies (see Deuteronomy 12:10–11). David realizes that the Deuteronomic covenant has been fulfilled. He expresses his desire to build a temple (see 2 Samuel 7:1–2; Psalm 132); however, God has other plans.

David can't build a house for the Lord—too much blood is on his hands from battle—but the *Lord* will build *David* a house! There are three levels of meaning of *house* (*bayith*): (1) *family:* God gives David a son; (2) *dynasty:* God promises David that a royal heir will reign on the throne of the kingdom forever; (3) *temple:* God will allow David's son Solomon to build the temple, the house of God (see 2 Samuel 7:13).

David as Liturgical Leader

God's family has expanded from a *marriage* (Adam), to a *household* (Noah), to a *tribe* (Abraham), to a *nation* (Moses) and finally now to a *kingdom* (David). The Davidic kingdom is more than a political entity; it is God's means of extending his covenant.

At Mount Sinai God called Israel to be a "kingdom of priests" (Exodus 19:6), but they failed to achieve this calling. Now God establishes the son of David on Jerusalem's Mount Zion as a priest-king through whom Israel's calling is restored.

David is a king, but he also aspires to *priestly* service: he wears a Levitical garment, he leads the procession of the ark of the covenant from the house of Obededom into the tabernacle in Jerusalem, he offers sacrifices, he blesses the people in the name of the Lord, and he serves the people bread, meat and wine (see 2 Samuel 6:14–19). He also writes numerous songs for use in Israel's worship, many of which are ascribed to him in the Book of Psalms.

God makes David a king and a priest. Not only does David conquer the land and rule as king, but he also receives the blueprint for the temple and its worship (see 1 Chronicles 28:19). He organizes the liturgical celebration, including the duties of the Levites, ministers and choirs in the tabernacle (see 1 Chronicles 15:16–24).

The Book of Leviticus describes thank offerings (see Leviticus 7:12–15), yet it is David who makes them a prominent aspect of Israel's liturgical life (see Psalms 22; 69; 100; 116). David commands the Levites to offer thank offerings (*todah*) perpetually before the ark (the sign of God's presence in the tabernacle). Here we have the first mention of perpetual adoration (see 1 Chronicles 16:37–42).

Jesus as the New David

The Davidic covenant is the final covenant between God and Israel. It is the "climax" of the Old Testament. Compare the key Davidic covenant text with the angel Gabriel's description of Jesus to Mary at the Annunciation:

2 Samuel 7:8–17	Luke 1:32–33
"a great name" (9)	"He will be great"
"he shall be my son" (14)	"will be called Son of the Most High"
"your throne shall be established" (16)	"God will give to him the throne of his father David"
"forever" (16)	"reign…forever"

There are seven primary and three secondary characteristics of the Davidic covenant we want to examine.

Primary Features of the Davidic Covenant. *The Son of David is the Son of God.* God swears that David's son will be God's son (see 2 Samuel 7:14; Psalm 2:7). On the day of his enthronement the Davidic king was anointed by a Levite. Once he was anointed, he was God's son. The Davidic king is thus called God's "first-born" (Psalm 89:27). In the Davidic king Israel's original calling finds partial fulfillment.

Firstborn Son	Priest-King
Israel: God's firstborn son (Exodus 4:22)	Kingdom of priests (Exodus 19:6)
David: God's firstborn son (Psalm 89:27)	King and priest (Psalm 110:1–4)
Jesus: the eternal Son of God (Hebrews 1:6)	The high priest who reigns in heaven (Hebrews 8:1)

The Davidic king is a "messiah." In Hebrew the word for "anointed one," *mashiach* [mah she' ah], means "messiah." The Davidic king was crowned in order to be enthroned; he was anointed by a Levitical priest in order to be consecrated. The royal anointing was associated with the reception of God's Spirit (see 1 Samuel 16:13). David (see Psalm 89:20–21), Solomon (see 1 Kings 1:32–40) and other Davidic kings (see 2 Kings 11:12; 23:30; 2 Chronicles 23:11) were all anointed.

Jesus is the true anointed one of God. The Greek word for "anointed one" is *Christos.* Jesus is the "son of David" according to the genealogy of Joseph (Matthew 1:1). Jesus is baptized by John the Baptist (a Levite), whose father is a priest (see Luke 1:5; John 1:32). Following Jesus' baptism, the Holy Spirit descends on him, and God declares Jesus to be his beloved Son (see Mark 1:9–11). Immediately following his baptism, Jesus announces the coming of the kingdom of God. He is thirty years old when he begins his ministry—the same age David was when he began to reign as king (see 2 Samuel 5:4; Luke 3:23).

The Davidic kingdom is international. God's covenant with Israel under Moses was national in scope; his covenant with David is international in scope. David's royal cabinet includes non-Israelites (see 1 Chronicles 11:11–12). Solomon establishes covenant treaties with other nations, like Tyre (see 1 Kings 5:1–12). The kingdom is not limited to nations around the land of Canaan. Psalm 72 describes Solomon's reign in universal terms (verses 8 and 11). God's covenant extends through the kingdom to all nations (see Psalm 2:8).

Jesus instructs the apostles to make disciples of "all nations" (Matthew 28:19). He commissions them to spread the gospel "to the end of the earth" (Acts 1:8; see 13:47).

The Davidic kingdom is located in Jerusalem. Jerusalem is the political capital for the Davidic kingdom, but Mount Zion in Jerusalem is to be the spiritual center of Israel, the place where nations will gather before God's presence. Psalm 87:5 states that peoples of all nations will be united to the Lord on Mount Zion.

On Mount Zion, in the Upper Room, Jesus establishes his reign when he institutes the Eucharist. In the same Upper Room his disciples receive the Holy Spirit on Pentecost. The author of the Letter to the Hebrews refers to the heavenly Jerusalem as Mount Zion, the city of the living God, our place of worship (see Hebrews 12:22–24).

The temple of Solomon is a place of worship. The temple is the place God chooses for his name to dwell (see 1 Kings 8:27–29). This fulfills Moses' prophecy in Deuteronomy 12:10–12. The temple is a place of prayer and worship for Israel and all of the nations.

God gives Israel an architectural sign that embodies the covenant. Moses makes a temporary "tent of meeting" (that is, tabernacle) for Israel alone to worship God (with no music) on Mount Sinai. Through David and Solomon God establishes his temple, which includes gentiles in its construction (see 1 Kings 5:1–12) and worship (see Luke 7:2–4). Here music also becomes integral to the worship of God.

Ancient Israel believed that the temple was built on a sacred rock, the foundation stone (*eben shetiyah* [eh vahn shet´ ee yah] in Hebrew) where Abraham offered Isaac (see 2 Chronicles 3:1). Just as the son of David (Solomon) built the temple on the foundation rock, so the Son of David (Jesus—one "greater than Solomon" in Matthew 12:42) will build the temple on Peter the rock (see Matthew 16:18). Jesus refers to his body as the temple when he predicts that the temple will be destroyed and three days later be rebuilt (see John 2:19–21). Jesus reigns now in the heavenly temple (see Hebrews 8:5).

God gives the king wisdom to build, to govern and to teach. God asks Solomon what he wants; Solomon asks for wisdom so that he will be able to govern a vast empire justly (see 1 Kings 3:5–12). This pleases God so much that he gives Solomon not only wisdom but also wealth and a long life (see 1 Kings 3:13–14, 28; 4:29). God gives Solomon wisdom to build and dedicate the temple (see 1 Kings 6; 8) and to instruct all nations in God's ways when they seek his wisdom (see 1 Kings 4:34; 10:1–10).

Solomon sends God's wisdom throughout the world. Wisdom literature—such as Proverbs, Ecclesiastes, Song of Solomon and Wisdom of Solomon—is attributed to him. These books are similar to "wisdom" books written by other ancient civilizations; but unlike the Torah, the wisdom books of Solomon don't contain the ritual laws peculiar to Israel. Thus the wisdom books communicate the universal moral and ethical norms for all the nations.

Jesus is the true Son of David through whom wisdom comes to the world (see 1 Corinthians 1:30). He instructs the nations in the ways of the Father. Through him God's Wisdom (the Holy Spirit) is given (see John 12:7–15).

The kingdom is an everlasting kingdom. David's kingdom is everlasting (see 2 Samuel 7:13; Psalm 89:36–37). The Davidic dynasty is the longest lasting dynasty in recorded history: from 1000 to 586 BC one of David's sons ruled in Jerusalem. No other kingdom has had an unbroken line of dynastic succession comparable to the Davidic dynasty.

But a four-hundred-year dynasty is not "everlasting," is it? In 586 BC it seems as though God's promise to David fails. The Davidic king is caught, and his sons are killed before him (see 2 Kings 25:7). But the prophets remind Israel of God's promise: the kingdom will be restored, and a son of David will reign.

In Jesus God's covenant oath is fulfilled. As the Son of David who reigns in heaven, Jesus transfers the kingdom to the heavenly Jerusalem. His kingdom is truly an everlasting kingdom!

Secondary Features of the Davidic Covenant. *Solomon establishes a throne for the queen mother.* Like other kings before and after him, Solomon has more than one wife but only one mother, Bathsheba. Solomon's mother is given a crown and reigns as queen (see 1 Kings 2:19). This exalted position continues throughout the Davidic line and is referred to as the *giberah* [gib' e rah].

Since Jesus is the King of Kings, his mother, Mary, is the chosen mother. She serves the kingdom of heaven in an exalted position.

The prime minister rules the kingdom as chief steward under the king. He is given *keys* that denote his *authority* and the *succession* involved in this position (see Isaiah 22:15–22).

Jesus establishes Peter as his prime minister in Matthew 16:19. Though Peter denies him three times (see Matthew 26:69–75), Jesus commissions Peter to lead the disciples when he appears to them on the beach (see John 21:15–19).

The todah (or "thank offering") becomes the primary liturgy celebrated in the temple (see Leviticus 7:11–15; 1 Chronicles 16). David wrote many *todah* or "thank offering" psalms, which follow a similar pattern of three stages. Psalm 50 illustrates these.

First, a person in a life-threatening situation cries out to God for deliverance and makes a voluntary vow to offer a sacrifice of thanksgiving upon being saved. "Offer to God a sacrifice of thanksgiving, / and pay your vows to the Most High; / and call upon me in the day of trouble" (Psalm 50:14–15).

Second, God promises to respond. "I will deliver you" (Psalm 50:15).

Third, the rescued individual offers a sacrifice in the temple and brings bread to be blessed. He gathers his family and friends and shares with them the con- secrated unleavened *bread* (the only time in the Old Testament when laypeople could eat consecrated bread) and a *cup* of wine, proclaiming the Lord's deliverance. "And you shall glorify me" (Psalm 50:15).

Through the *todah* Israel learned to offer afflictions to God in thanksgiving. The psalms explain that this act of thanksgiving is what the Lord truly wants (see Psalm 69:30–31).

The Greek word for thanksgiving is *eucharistia* [you car ist ee' uh], from which we get the word *Eucharist*. Jesus offers himself through the Church's eucharistic offering. In this offering we eat consecrated bread and proclaim Christ's death and resurrection over the cup. We also offer ourselves.

The Kingdom Established

One way in which David does not resemble Jesus is in his sin (see 2 Samuel 11). David is not where he is supposed to be: He remains at home instead of leading the troops in battle. He lingers at his window, watching Bathsheba bathe on her roof. He longs for her, though she is the wife of Uriah, a Hittite warrior and one of David's most trusted soldiers.

David invites Bathsheba into his bedchamber, and he commits adultery with her. When she conceives, David tries to cover up his sin. When the cover-up fails, David sets Uriah up to be killed in battle.

The prophet Nathan confronts David and pronounces God's judgment: The sword will never depart out of David's house, and his child will die. David repents deeply, praying Psalm 51, the great psalm of contrition. Then he marries Bathsheba.

When Bathsheba delivers their son, he is very ill, and he dies shortly afterward. David and Bathsheba comfort each other and conceive another son, Solomon, who becomes David's heir to the throne.

Shortly after Solomon's coronation the three promises made to Abraham in Genesis 12:2–3 are fulfilled: *land and nationhood* (see 1 Kings 4:21); *a great name through a royal dynasty* (see 2 Samuel 7:9; 1 Kings 4:20–21; see Genesis 22:17–18); and *worldwide blessing* through God's temple and wisdom (see Psalm 72:17). The movement from Moses and the nation of Israel to David's kingdom—from Sinai to Zion—is complete:

Moses and Israel	David's Kingdom
Mount Sinai in the wildernes	Mount Zion in Jerusalem
Exclusive, national	Inclusive, international
Tent for Israel's worship	Temple for all to worship
Sin offerings	Thank offerings
Torah, law of God	*Hokmah,* wisdom of Solomon

The Fall of the Kingdom and the Promise of Restoration

In anticipation of future kings of Israel, Moses gives three warnings in Deuteronomy 17:16–17: do not multiply *weapons, wealth* or *wives*. King Solomon, at first, leads the people in wisdom. Tragically, however, he fails to heed all three warnings: he multiplies *weapons* (horses used for battle) (see 2 Chronicles 9:25, 28) and *wealth* (see 1 Kings 10:14, 23–25, 27). His political alliances through marriage result in seven hundred *wives* and three hundred concubines. They in turn draw Solomon's heart away from the Lord (see 1 Kings 11:1–5).

Due to Solomon's sin God allows the kingdom to be divided after his death. The ten northern tribes rebel against the Davidic king and form the northern kingdom of Israel. The two southern tribes (Judah and Benjamin) form the southern kingdom of Judah, and a Davidic king continues to rule them (see 1 Kings 11:9–40).

In 722 BC the Assyrians conquer the northern kingdom of Israel and permanently scatter the people among the nations. In 586 BC the Babylonians capture the southern kingdom of Judah after they destroy Jerusalem and the temple. After seventy years in exile, the "Judahites" (or "Judeans" or "Jews") return to their land and slowly rebuild the temple under Zarubbabel and then Ezra and Nehemiah. However, they still struggle against their enemies.

In the Mosaic covenant Israel has a twofold administration. God establishes the Levites to uphold the Law and to co-administer the civil codes with the elders in Israel. God also calls judges—men and women—to rescue the Israelites and rule them by the Spirit.

Something similar happens in the Davidic covenant. Although the Davidic king is the political leader of the people, responsible for the Law, God sends his Spirit upon the prophets—men like Nathan, Isaiah and Jeremiah. The prophets foretell God's restoration of the Davidic kingdom through a messiah. Isaiah 53:4–6 states that the Messiah will not be triumphant by winning a great military battle. On the contrary he will suffer greatly, but through his sufferings he will atone for sins. The Messiah will offer himself as a sacrifice to God. Jeremiah 31:31–34 explains that through the Messiah, God will establish a "new covenant" to restore his family. Through the new covenant God's plan to make us his covenant family will be fulfilled (see Jeremiah 32:36–41).

The future Son of David will defeat evil once and for all. He will restore the kingdom as God's worldwide covenant family. The next lesson will focus on the final stage in God's covenant plan, the new covenant. God fulfills all of his Old Testament promises in Christ—the Son of David, the Messiah!

Review Questions for Personal Study

1. What is the twofold role of David? In what way is he a king and a priest?
2. What are the seven major characteristics of the Davidic covenant?
3. How do these characteristics relate to Christ and his work?
4. What role do the prophets play, and how does it relate to the role of the judges in the Mosaic covenant?
5. How do the prophets describe the victory of the coming Messiah?

Recommended Verses to Memorize

Jeremiah 31:31–33

Matthew 1:1

Luke 1:32–33

Jesus: Fulfillment of the Promises

Salvation history reveals how God works through the covenants of the Old Testament to make us his family. In the person and work of Jesus Christ in the new covenant, God fulfills his promises to Adam, Abraham, Moses and David. This lesson highlights Jesus' perfect fulfillment of these Old Testament types.

In Christ we have a new creation, a new exodus and a new kingdom.

The New Moses

Jesus' birth parallels Moses' birth. Both Jesus and Moses are born during the reign of a ruthless king; both tyrants kill other Hebrew male children ("the slaughter of the innocents"). Both Jesus and Moses find safety in Egypt. Finally, after the tyrant's death, both come out of Egypt, pass through waters and are led into the desert.

Ministry.   Jesus fasts for forty days and forty nights, as did Moses. Jesus is tempted by Satan in the desert, just as Israel was tested in the wilderness. To rebuke the devil Jesus cites the very passages from Deuteronomy 6—8 where Moses explained to Israel why they failed the test they faced in the wilderness. Deuteronomy 8:3 says the people do "not live by bread alone." Deuteronomy 6:16 says, "You shall not put the LORD your God to the test." Deuteronomy 6:13 exhorts them to serve God alone. Jesus succeeds where Israel failed.

After his forty-day fast, Jesus begins his public ministry by declaring the new covenant law on a mountain (see Matthew 5—7), the Sermon on the Mount. After his forty days' fast, Moses also gave Israel the law of God from a mountain—Mount Sinai. Jesus' mission is to fulfill God's Word—*not* to abolish the Law and the prophets (see Matthew 5:17). Thus he does not relax the law of Moses; he *internalizes* it and *intensifies* it. For example, while Moses commanded Israel not to commit adultery, Jesus states that anyone who even looks lustfully at a woman commits adultery with her in his heart (see Matthew 5:31–32).

What Moses gave is great; what Jesus gives is greater (see John 1:17). Jesus challenges the Israelites to allow the Scriptures (and Moses' writings in particular) to bear witness to him (see John 5:39, 46–47).

Signs and Miracles. Throughout his life and ministry, Jesus works signs and miracles. The Gospel of John records Jesus' first "sign" at the wedding feast at Cana (see John 2:1–11). There Jesus turns water in the stone jars into wine. Moses' first sign was turning water into blood, including water in "vessels of stone" (Exodus 7:19).

Another sign Jesus performs is the miraculous feeding of the crowds (see John 6:5–14). Jesus multiplies the loaves of bread and the fish so that twelve baskets are left over (symbolizing the twelve tribes of Israel). Moses fed Israel with miraculous bread from heaven (see Exodus 16:2–30). Unlike Moses, however, Jesus himself is the true Bread from heaven (see John 6:32, 35).

Jesus also demonstrates his power and mercy through healing the sick. An example of this is his curing of a leper (see Matthew 8:2–3). Moses also prayed for a leper, his sister Miriam, and his prayer resulted in her healing (see Numbers 12:10–15).

Friends and Enemies. Though Jesus and Moses both have the Law and miraculous power, they choose coworkers to assist them in caring for God's people. Jesus appoints twelve apostles (see Luke 6:13–16), and later he appoints seventy disciples (see Luke 10:1). Moses also chooses twelve tribal princes (see Numbers 13) and appoints seventy elders to assist him (see Numbers 11). Jesus' inner circle includes Peter, James and John; Moses' inner circle includes Nadab, Abihu and Aaron (see Exodus 24:1; 28:1).

Throughout his ministry the Jewish leaders oppose Jesus. When Jesus casts out demons, the Pharisees accuse him of being in league with Satan (see Matthew 9:32–34). They even plot to kill him. Here again is a parallel with Moses, who was opposed by Israel's leaders throughout the Books of Exodus and Numbers (see, for example, Numbers 12:1–2).

Transfigured on a Mountain. The Transfiguration underlines Jesus' role as the new Moses. Jesus goes up a mountain with three companions (see Luke 9:28), as did Moses (see Exodus 24:1, 15). Jesus' appearance is transfigured in the midst of God's presence in the glory-cloud (see Luke 9:29), as was Moses' (see Exodus 34:29–35). Jesus speaks to Moses (the giver of the Law) and Elijah (the greatest prophet) about his "departure" (that is, his "exodus"—Luke 9:30–31).

The evangelists clearly see Jesus as a New Moses who leads a new exodus and gives a new law.

The Passover Celebrated and Fulfilled

The Gospels show us how Jesus celebrates and transforms the Passover into the Eucharist (see Matthew 26:26–29). Jesus sends Peter and John to make preparations for the Passover (see Luke 22:7–13). He institutes the Eucharist as a memorial (see Luke 22:19, "in remembrance"), just as the Passover was a "memorial" (see Exodus 12:14). After they finish eating, Jesus tells his apostles to "watch and pray" (see Matthew 26:38, 41); this reflects the Passover as "a night of watching" (Exodus 12:42). Jesus blesses the cup, calling it the "blood of the covenant" (Matthew 26:28), reminiscent of Moses' sealing the covenant with Israel with the blood of the sacrifice, which he called "the blood of the covenant" (Exodus 24:8).

The Gospel of John describes how Jesus fulfills the Passover through his passion and death (see John 19). The soldiers take Jesus to be crucified at the sixth hour—the hour the high priest begins to slaughter Passover lambs (see John 19:14). John explains that the soldiers do not break Jesus' legs—fulfilling the prescription that the Passover lamb have no broken bones or blemishes (see John 19:32–36; Exodus 12:46). Further, John notes that Jesus' seamless garment is not torn, like the robe worn by the high priest (see John 19:23; Exodus 28:32). Finally, the soldiers raise a sponge of vinegar to Jesus' mouth on a hyssop branch, which is the kind of branch used to sprinkle the blood of the Passover lamb (see John 19:29; Exodus 12:21–23).

All of this demonstrates that the Eucharist—which is the new Passover—and Calvary are inseparable. They are one and the same sacrifice!

What Jesus begins in the Upper Room he concludes on the cross. The bread becomes Jesus' body, which is "given for you" (Luke 22:19). The wine is Jesus' blood, which is "poured out for you" (Luke 22:20). Here Jesus evokes the image of the Levitical priests who were instructed by Moses to "pour out" the blood of the sacrifice (Exodus 29:12; Leviticus 4:7). Through the Eucharist Jesus offers himself to the Father (see Isaiah 53:3–12).

The New Adam in the Garden

While the first Adam was disobedient in the garden, Jesus (the New Adam) goes into a garden and prays, "Your will be done" (Matthew 26:42). His obedience undoes what Adam's disobedience has done.

Adam triggered the curse of the covenant: He was ashamed and naked (see Genesis 3:10); his work became toilsome and not always fruitful (see Genesis 3:18); his labor was difficult and sweat-producing (see Genesis 3:19); and his physical death was inevitable (see Genesis 3:19). Jesus bears the covenant curses redemptively: His sweat is like drops of blood (see Luke 22:44); he wears a crown of thorns (see Matthew 27:29); he is stripped (see Matthew 27:31). Jesus goes to the cross, which is called the "Tree of Life" in the early Church (see Genesis 2:9; Acts 5:30). When he falls into the sleep of death, his bride, the Church, is formed from his side (see John 19:26–35).

The work of salvation is not complete with Jesus' death for our sins. We are saved by the cross *and* the Resurrection. "Jesus our Lord...was put to death for our trespasses and raised for our justification" (Romans 4:24–25). Without the Resurrection we could not be saved.

The Resurrection is more than resuscitation from the dead or the vindication of an innocent man. In his resurrection Jesus' humanity is divinized—glorified (see *CCC*, 651–655); and by uniting ourselves to him, we share in his glorified humanity. In a very real sense, the Resurrection is the climax of God's covenant plan (see 1 Corinthians 15:20–22, 42–45).

On Easter Sunday Jesus rises from the dead and appears in the garden (see John 20:15). Because of their sin man and woman were banished from the garden. On Easter Sunday Jesus restores humanity, announcing the new creation in a garden. And this grace has entered the world, in part, through the humility of the new Eve, Mary, untying the knot of Eve's disobedience.

The Son of Abraham

On the third day the Father receives his only beloved Son back from the dead. Through Jesus' resurrection God fulfills the oath he swore to Abraham in Genesis 22:18 to bless all nations through Abraham's seed.

Little did Abraham realize that God was using him and his son Isaac to foreshadow the way this covenant oath would be fulfilled. When Abraham offered his only beloved son on Mount Moriah, he told Isaac: "God will provide himself the lamb" (Genesis 22:8). Abraham believed that Isaac was the son of promise and that God could resurrect him if need be (see Hebrews 11:19).

The first verse in the New Testament identifies Jesus as "the son of Abraham." Jesus is the only beloved Son of the Father (see John 3:16). He offers himself as a sacrifice to God on Calvary (one of the peaks of Moriah). Like Isaac, he carries the wood of the sacrifice up the mountain, and there God provides himself as the Lamb. On the third day the Father raises his Son from the dead—just as Abraham received his son back on the third day (see Genesis 22:4). In short, through his death and resurrection, Jesus fulfills God's promise to Abraham to bless all the nations (see Galatians 3:13–14).

The Son of David

Matthew's Gospel reflects on the apostles' experiences with Christ in a new light—in the divine light of the Spirit. They not only understand Jesus as the New Moses and the Son of Abraham, but they also see Jesus as the Son of David come to fulfill the Davidic covenant.

Matthew's Gospel begins with Jesus' genealogy: He is the "son of David" (Matthew 1:1). Jesus' birthplace is the same as David's, Bethlehem (see 1 Samuel 16:1; Matthew 2:1).

Jesus is the "anointed one," the true Davidic king. In the last lesson we saw how the Davidic king was always anointed by a Levite (see 1 Kings 1:34; 2 Kings 11:12; 23:30; 2 Chronicles 23:11). Matthew 3 records that Jesus was baptized by John the Baptist, a Levite, and "after the baptism which John preached...God anointed Jesus of Nazareth with the Holy Spirit and with power" (Acts 10:37–38).

Once anointed, the king was declared the adopted son of God (see Psalm 2:7). Already the eternal Son of God, Jesus becomes the Son of David by God's grace and mercy. John the Baptist hears the Father's declaration, "This is my beloved Son" (Matthew 3:17).

Jesus begins his public ministry by preaching "the gospel of the kingdom" (Matthew 4:23). This is his primary theme. His Sermon on the Mount begins with eight beatitudes that begin and end with the promise, "Theirs is the kingdom of heaven" (Matthew 5:3, 10).

In Matthew 6 Jesus gives us the Our Father, in which we are to pray, "Thy kingdom come..." (Matthew 6:10). Throughout the Sermon on the Mount

Jesus emphasizes the fatherhood of God, mentioning it seventeen times in three chapters. He also urges the people to seek the kingdom above all (see Matthew 6:33).

In Matthew 7 Jesus describes the ideal disciple in terms reminiscent of Solomon. Solomon built the temple on the foundation stone; here we have the "wise man" who "built his house upon the rock" (Matthew 7:24). Jesus tells us that his wisdom is greater than that of Solomon (see Matthew 12:42).

Solomon taught wisdom through proverbs and parables; in Matthew 13 Jesus teaches about the kingdom through seven parables. He shows us that saints and sinners make up the Church, the kingdom in this world; only on the last day will God separate the "wheat" from the "chaff" (Matthew 13:24–30; 36–43). Further, the Church-kingdom is not an earthly political institution; rather it is a "treasure" hidden in the world. Though it is of the greatest good, the world does not recognize its value (see Matthew 13:45–46).

Matthew records Jesus' ministry to gentiles as well as Israelites: He heals the centurion's son (see Matthew 8:5–13) and a Canaanite woman (see Matthew 15:22–28), and he casts a demon out of the Syrophoenician woman's daughter (see Mark 7:24–30). The crowds that gather to hear him include people from outside Israel, "from about Tyre and Sidon" (Mark 3:8).

Jesus does not simply "take" the kingdom away to heaven. The kingdom is present on earth through the ministry of the apostles, especially through Peter (see Matthew 16:18–19). The Greek word for "assembly" (*ekklesia*) translates to "Church" in English. Just as Solomon built the temple on the rock, so Jesus builds the Church on Peter the "rock."

Jesus also gives Peter the "keys" of the kingdom. Keys in the Old Testament symbolized the prime minister's authority in the kingdom: He was given the authority to "shut" and "open," and he was called to be a "father" (see Isaiah 22:20, 22). Jesus employs similar language when he gives Peter the keys: He gives Peter the authority to "bind" and "loose" (Matthew 16:19). Peter is also called to be a father, as *pope* means "father." Thus, through the Church's ministry, the kingdom Christ established in heaven is present now on earth.

The Gospel writers understood that on Palm Sunday, Jesus as the Son of David comes to the city of David to restore the kingdom of David (see Mark 11:10; Luke 19:38). Instead of riding triumphantly into Jerusalem, however, Jesus arrives humbly on a donkey—just as Solomon did (see Matthew 21:6–7; 1 Kings 1:38). The people shout, "Hosanna to the Son of David!" (Matthew

21:9), but Jesus' triumph as the Davidic king will not come through political or military strength.

The Kingdom Banquet

In Luke's Gospel the Passover meal Jesus celebrates is intimately connected to the coming of the kingdom. Jesus tells the apostles, "I shall not eat it until it is fulfilled in the kingdom of God" (Luke 22:16), and, "I shall not drink of the fruit of the vine until the kingdom of God comes" (Luke 22:18). He also tells them that they will eat and drink at his table and sit on thrones in the kingdom (see Luke 22:30).

The disciples' dispute about how the kingdom will be administered is placed in the middle of this passage. Jesus challenges them not to lord authority over others but rather to follow his example as a king who serves at the table (see Luke 22:27).

Jesus not only institutes the Eucharist but also ordains the priests who will follow his example and offer this sacrifice "in remembrance" of him. *Remembrance* is liturgical language. As the apostles continue with Jesus through his trials, they receive a call: Jesus appoints (or "covenants") them to imitate him as king, to exercise royal authority and to extend the kingdom—all of which they will do as they offer the Eucharist. It is significant that the only kingdom "covenanted" in Scripture is the kingdom of David (see Psalm 89:19–37). This is the kingdom that foreshadows Christ's kingdom.

In the last lesson we saw how David moved the thank offering (the *todah*) to the center of Israel's liturgical life. We also saw how *todah* (when translated into Greek) is *Eucharist,* meaning "thanksgiving." On the cross Jesus prays Psalm 22—a *todah* psalm. He appeals to God to vindicate him, to save him. Though he begins with the first verse speaking of abandonment, the psalm concludes with praise to God for his deliverance.

The Last Supper is Jesus' *todah* meal. Through the Eucharist we share in the *todah* of our Davidic priest-king: We proclaim Christ's death and resurrection, and we offer ourselves through Christ's offering. Furthermore, through the Eucharist we enter into the kingdom, the family of God—the Trinity—and thus God's covenant plan is accomplished. The logic of the kingdom is the logic of the Trinity: life-giving love.

As we offer ourselves to God in the Eucharist, we receive a foretaste of heaven. Wherever the King is, there is the kingdom; and wherever the Eucharist is, there is the King!

The Kingdom Restored

After his resurrection Jesus appears to the apostles, and then he remains with them for forty days. Acts 1:3 tells us that he speaks to them about "the kingdom of God." The apostles were eager for the restoration of the kingdom (see Acts 1:6). Jesus explains that the kingdom will be restored when they receive the Holy Spirit. The apostles will be "witnesses in Jerusalem and...Judea and Samaria and to the end of the earth" (Acts 1:8). This is a map of the Davidic kingdom under Solomon. (Psalm 72:8 describes Solomon's reign extending "to the ends of the earth.")

Thus, through the ministry of the Church in Acts, the kingdom is restored. The Book of Acts begins with Jesus and then Saint Peter proclaiming the kingdom. In his inaugural sermon at Pentecost, Peter uses the Psalms to show how the Resurrection and the Ascension represent the fulfillment of the Davidic covenant (see Acts 2:29–36):

- The Lord fulfills David's prayer for preservation from death—not in David, since he died, but in the Messiah (see Psalm 16:8–11).

- The Lord swore to David that he would establish an everlasting kingdom through him; Jesus' heavenly reign fulfills this promise (see Psalm 89:3–4; 132:11–12).

- The Lord established the Davidic Messiah at his right hand; through the Ascension Jesus is seated at the Father's right hand (see Psalm 110:1; Mark 16:19).

At the center of the Book of Acts is the Jerusalem Council, where the apostles deal with the admission of gentiles into the Church. Saint James recognizes that the kingdom of David is restored, for Israelites as well as for gentiles, through the Church (see Acts 15:12–21).

Saint Paul speaks at Antioch in Acts 13, and he uses the Old Testament to show how the Resurrection and Ascension represent Jesus' heavenly enthronement. Psalm 2, which he quotes, was originally an enthronement psalm, celebrating God's anointing of the Davidic king and his adoption of him as his son.

Acts ends with Saint Paul's preaching of the kingdom in Rome (see Acts 28:31). He addresses the Christians in Rome (Israelites and gentiles) with a declaration of Jesus as the son of David and the Son of God (see Romans 1:1–4). Through God's kingdom his covenant is extended to all nations.

Through the Resurrection the Davidic king conquers death, fulfilling God's oath to David to establish his kingdom forever (see 2 Samuel 7:13). Through the Ascension Jesus transfers the kingdom to heaven. Hebrews 12:22–23 notes that we "have come to Mount Zion and to...the heavenly Jerusalem." Established in heaven, the kingdom never will be shaken.

Review Questions for Personal Study

1. Matthew identifies Jesus as the son of which two important Old Testament figures? What is their significance?

2. What is the major theme of Jesus' ministry? How does this theme reflect the fulfillment of God's covenant promises in the Old Testament?

3. In what ways does the kingdom restored by Jesus surpass the kingdom of David and Solomon?

4. How is the Eucharist the new Passover?

5. What is the connection between the Passover Jesus celebrates in the Upper Room and the crucifixion?

6. How is the kingdom of God present in the Church's eucharistic celebration?

7. How does Jesus bear the curses Adam and Eve incurred?

8. How does he bear the curse Israel incurred so that God's promise to Abraham can be fulfilled?

9. How is the Eucharist a *todah* sacrifice for us?

10. How is Jesus the New Adam? the Son of Abraham? the New Moses? the true Davidic King?

Recommended Verses to Memorize

Luke 22:19–20

John 3:16

Acts 1:8

Postscript

Journey Through Scripture is a series of Bible studies produced in conjunction with the St. Paul Center for Biblical Theology. *Genesis to Jesus* is the first study in this series. Other studies in the series include *The Bible and the Mass, The Bible and Mary* and *The Bible and the Church.*

Seminars are scheduled at various times of the year in different parts of the country to train presenters of these materials. In turn, presenters lead these studies in their homes or parishes. For more information on these studies and other materials produced by the St. Paul Center, please go to our Web site, www.salvationhistory.com.

The St. Paul Center for Biblical Theology is committed to the dual goals of increasing biblical literacy for all Catholics and biblical fluency for all clergy.

Notes

Introduction

1. Saint Jerome, *Commentariorum in Isaiam libri xviii* prol.: J.P. Migne, ed., *Patrologia Latina* (Paris: 1841–1855), 24, 17b; see *Dei Verbum*, 25; *CCC*, 133.

2. Saint Augustine, *Quaestiones in Heptateuchum*, 2, 73, *Patrologia Latina*, 34, 623; see *Dei Verbum,*16, *CCC*, 129.

Lesson One

1. Quoting Saint Bernard, *S. missus est moninis*, 4, 11: *Patrologia Latina*, 183, 86.

2. Saint Irenaeus, "Against Heresies," book 1, chapter 10, n. 3, in *Early Christian Fathers*, ed. Cyril C. Richardson (New York: Macmillan, 1972), p. 361.

Lesson Three

1. See Scott Hahn, *A Father Who Keeps His Promises: God's Covenant Love in Scripture* (Cincinnati: Servant, 1998), p. 90.